Lighting and colour
for hospital design

London: TSO

NHS
Estates

Published by TSO (The Stationery Office) and available from:

Online

www.tso.co.uk/bookshop

Mail, Telephone, Fax & E-mail
TSO
PO Box 29, Norwich NR3 1GN
Telephone orders/General enquiries 0870 600 5522
Fax orders 0870 600 5533
E-mail book.orders@tso.co.uk

TSO Shops

123 Kingsway, London WC2B 6PQ
020 7242 6393 Fax 020 7242 6394
68–69 Bull Street, Birmingham B4 6AD
0121 236 9696 Fax 0121 236 9699
9–21 Princess Street, Manchester M60 8AS
0161 834 7201 Fax 0161 833 0634
16 Arthur Street, Belfast BT1 4GD
028 9023 8451 Fax 028 9023 5401
18–19 High Street, Cardiff CF10 1PT
029 2039 5548 Fax 029 2038 4347
71 Lothian Road, Edinburgh EH3 9AZ
0870 606 5566 Fax 0870 606 5588

TSO Accredited Agents

(see Yellow Pages)

and through good booksellers

ISBN 0-11-322491-5

First published 2004

Printed in the United Kingdom for The Stationery Office

Cover photograph: 'Colour Changer 3'
Remote Controlled Colour Changing Wallwashing Light
Unit
Courtesy of Elga Niemann, Colour Design Research
Centre, South Bank University

The paper used in the printing of this document
(Revive Silk) is 75% made from 100% de-inked post-
consumer waste, the remaining 25% being mill broke
and virgin fibres. Recycled papers used in its
production are a combination of Totally Chlorine Free
(TCF) and Elemental Chlorine Free (ECF). It is
recyclable and biodegradable and is an NAPM and
Eugropa approved recycled grade.

"I am inclined to think that the majority of cheerful cases is to be found among those who are not confined to one room, whatever they are suffering, and that the majority of depressed cases will be seen among those subjected to a long monotony of objects around them. A nervous frame really suffers as much from this as the digestive organs suffer from long monotony of diet. The effect on sickness of beautiful objects, on variety of objects and especially brilliancy of colours, is hardly to be appreciated. Such cravings are usually called the "fancies" of patients but these "fancies" are the most valuable indication of that which is necessary for their recovery. People say that the effect is only on the mind. It is no such thing. The effect is on the body too. Little as we know about the way in which we are affected by form and colour and light, we do know this: that they have an actual and physical effect. Variety of form and brilliance of colour in the objects presented to patients are an actual means of recovery"

Florence Nightingale

Foreword

Lighting and colour are particularly important in the built environment. Our research in airports and railway stations has shown that the psychological power of colour and control of lighting can influence the mood of people who may be anxious, disoriented or over-emotional.

Thus, when talking about the hospital environment, how much more important lighting and colour becomes. People are likely to remain in hospital for longer. Their anxieties might well be much the same, although stretched over a longer period, and they will probably feel generally unwell.

Here is a definitive and functional publication bringing together all aspects of colour and lighting needed for contemporary hospital design. It is a user-friendly document, for reference early in a building project, which can be fully understood by both professionals and lay people alike.

It will be of positive value, and I see it taking a natural part of the evidence-based programme being undertaken by the NHS.

Straightforward guidance has been needed for a long time and this publication clearly provides it.

Jane Priestman OBE
(BAA, British Rail) Design Management Consultant

Executive summary

This guidance document was written jointly by BRE and the Colour Design Research Centre at London South Bank University as part of a Department of Health (NHS Estates) funded project "Lighting and Colour Design for Hospital Environments". It covers the visual environment in hospitals and the use of appropriate colour design and lighting. It will be of interest to anyone involved in designing, refurbishing or maintaining hospital environments, particularly NHS specifiers, design teams and facilities managers. It includes a review of published work, visits to hospitals and interviews with designers, facilities managers, medical staff and patients.

THE VISUAL ENVIRONMENT

The quality of the visual environment has a positive effect on the occupant's feeling of well-being and in the case of hospitals and healthcare buildings this can affect staff performance and patient recovery. The cost of hospital staff and patient treatment is considerable; therefore, measures to maximise performance through improved environments will generally be cost-effective.

For these reasons, it is essential to consider lighting and colour design at the early stages of specifying and designing a building. Only then can a truly integrated approach to the visual environment be undertaken. It may be difficult, disruptive or costly to make changes once a hospital is in use.

Hospitals have a wide range of users (section 1.2) with different requirements, from the elderly to the very young. A well-designed visual environment can be particularly helpful to patients with partial sight.

COLOUR DESIGN AND INTERIORS

Colour (chapter 2) can play a major role in creating accessible environments. Surface textures and choice of materials provide visual and tactile clues to help people with poor vision use a building. Colour contrast can identify obstacles and hardware that might prove difficult to negotiate. Features of a building which create tonal detail or shadows can also aid the visually impaired. Well-designed, ambient environments will have transitions of lighting and colour design to allow the eye to adapt to changes in lighting levels.

The appearance and ambience of a building interior at night can be very different from daytime. It can be a frightening prospect to those with poor vision, whether a patient, member of staff or visitor. Landmarks or surfaces may not have enough contrast, colour-design highlighting or lighting to demarcate boundaries, assist wayfinding or identify potential obstacles.

LIGHTING AND DAYLIGHTING

Windows (section 3.1) are of key importance; as well as natural light, they provide an outlook, contact with the outside and access to sunlight about which patients are extremely positive. Windows should therefore be sized and positioned to provide a view out, regardless of location, as well as a reasonable average daylight factor. Good, controllable solar shading is essential. The colour and materials of window treatments such as blinds or curtains needs to be chosen with care to enhance the interiors or control glare (section 2.4).

An electric lighting installation (section 3.2) serves a number of needs; some are obvious, such as being able to see to move around safely or to carry out tasks which might be easy or complex.

Lighting has a considerable effect on the appearance of a space. The visual appearance of the lit space also applies to the way lighting equipment integrates with the architectural design and the physical elements of the building. It is equally important to ensure that electric light integrates with daylight.

For both lighting and colour design, a proper maintenance plan needs to be drawn up at the design stage, and carried out at regular intervals, to ensure that the quality of the visual environment remains high following installation or refurbishment.

Energy efficiency has a direct influence on running costs. The use of efficient lamps, ballasts and luminaires, coupled with appropriate lighting controls, can be highly cost-effective and help to meet energy targets for the NHS.

During the planning stage, it is essential to consider the running costs over the life of the installation as well as its capital cost. Lighting installation costs, even those involving high quality equipment, will be tiny compared with the cost of staff and medical equipment. If high quality lighting makes just a small improvement on the performance of the hospital, in terms of either staff productivity or patient recovery rates, then it will be a price worth paying.

THE HOSPITAL ENVIRONMENT

Chapter 4 of the guide deals with the design of specific areas: general (public) areas (section 4.2), circulation areas (section 4.3) and care areas (wards) (section 4.4). Specialist medical areas such as operating theatres are not covered in this guide.

For general areas and circulation areas (sections 4.2, 4.3) there are two priorities: to provide a pleasant environment for all hospital users, and to help and guide them as they move through the hospital.

Lighting design will concentrate on the appearance of spaces with enough light on walls and ceilings. Spaces will be more pleasant if daylight and views out are available.

Even in general areas, there is a surprising range of visual tasks; staff and users will need to be able to see to perform these tasks and to move around the building.

Hospitals must have emergency escape lighting to switch on automatically in a power failure. In some areas of a hospital, it will be necessary to provide stand-by lighting to enable procedures to be continued or shut down safely.

Sometimes a relatively minor change to the colour design or lighting of spaces can solve an ongoing, apparently insurmountable, problem (for example, extra lighting on walls with accent colour to brighten up a gloomy area). Colour design and lighting consultants can often pinpoint the reason why a place does not "feel" right. For example, a change of floor colour from light to dark or vice-versa can affect a whole area dramatically. Section 5.1 of the guide is intended to help here. It enables the facilities manager to troubleshoot common difficulties, suggesting appropriate solutions.

CONCLUSION

A properly designed visual environment, with the appropriate use of colour and lighting, will have important benefits in hospitals (see section 5.2). A relatively small investment in good, thoughtful colour and lighting design may reap major dividends over many years for patients, staff and visitors.

Acknowledgements

This report would not have been possible without the work undertaken by Nilgun Camgöz (LSBU), Louise Holgate (LSBU), Sarah Hill (Schoolworks & LSBU) and Jenny Little (LSBU) who are thanked for all their valuable field research and contributions. Additional support has been provided by Anthony Slater and Mike Perry (BRE) who managed some of the work and Emma Dewey (BRE) who organised hospital visits. Elga Niemann (LSBU) provided research, design and technical assistance, Guillaume Steadman (LSBU) for technical support on the hospital visits and Glen Manley (LSBU) and Ian Butler (LSBU) for CAD visualisations.

This report was funded by the Department of Health through the NHS Estates research programme. We would like to thank Jonathan Millman of NHS Estates for his advice and guidance. Additional funding was provided for photography and hospital visits by the Colour Design Research Centre at South Bank University.

The research was supported by an Advisory Panel comprising NHS Estates specialists, representatives of care organisations, accessible environments, patients associations, and manufacturers, hospital architects, designers and experts in the field. The Advisory Panel have provided help and advice and comments on an early draft of this guide.

Our very special thanks go to the large number of hospital staff, including facilities managers, nurses, doctors and ancillary staff, who gave up their valuable time to discuss colour design and lighting and to show us round their hospitals, providing a wealth of valuable comment and feedback. This report would not have been possible without their contributions. The hospitals are listed here:

1. Allgemeines Kranken Haus, Vienna, Austria
2. Bradford Royal Infirmary, West Yorkshire
3. Brighton General, Sussex
4. Bristol Royal Hospital
5. Southend, BUPA, Essex
6. Charing Cross, London
7. Chelsea & Westminster, London
8. Darent Valley
9. Derriford, Plymouth
10. Edinburgh Royal Infirmary
11. Great Ormond St Children's Hospital
12. Guys and St Thomas's – London Bridge
13. Guys and St Thomas's – Westminster
14. Kingston upon Thames, Surrey
15. North Middlesex
16. Poole, Dorset
17. St George's, Tooting, London
18. St Peter's, Chertsey, Surrey
19. Surrey County, Guildford
20. West Dorset General, Dorchester
21. Whipps Cross, London
22. Winchester, Hampshire

Contents

1. Background

1.1 Introduction

This publication provides guidance on the use of light and colour design in hospitals. It complements the CIBSE Lighting Guide: 'Hospitals and healthcare buildings' [1.1]. In particular, it is concerned with public spaces, which include the entrance and reception areas, circulation spaces and hospital wards. It does not consider the specialist clinical areas.

The guide has been produced to aid design teams, the hospital trusts that commission a facility and also the people who are responsible for its operation and maintenance.

Of all the human senses, vision is by far the most powerful in providing information about the world around us [1.2]. For the visual process to be effective, there needs to be good lighting to enable people to carry out tasks which can range from the relatively simple to the highly complex. It also informs us about the environment around us, not just in an objective way by determining things such as a room's shape, size and colouring but by creating a psychological sensation which can induce feelings of comfort, security, stimulation and much more [1.3].

The visual environment is formed by the interaction of its physical elements and the light that illuminates it. Thoughtful use of colour application can achieve so much in interior design. However, it is the nature of the physical elements and of the illumination together with the interaction between them that will determine its quality. Colour has a vital role here in enhancing the environment and providing information and spatial orientation, helping occupants make sense of their surroundings. Aesthetically, it can provide attractive, pleasing conditions for patients, visitors and staff.

There is some evidence (chapters 2 and 3) that the design of the visual environment, particularly with regard to the composition of light and colour, can have a positive effect on the well-being of the occupants [1.4–1.6]. For example, in some hospitals, it has been found that the quality of the visual environment has had a positive effect on the recovery rate of patients and of the effectiveness of staff, although research evidence is often limited. Nevertheless, this aspect of design should not be overlooked.

The physical aspects of the design of a building are the responsibility of the architect and the interior designer, if one is appointed. They in turn may appoint a specialist lighting designer as well as a colour design consultant to help ensure that a high quality visual environment is achieved. In a hospital, this is particularly important because of its function, its many requirements and the different people it serves.

The application of colour and design to patients' accommodation should take account of the emotional and psychological factors which can affect their well-being. This should include the likes and dislikes of user groups of all age groups and cultures. The primary objective is to achieve a friendly and welcoming atmosphere with variety and interest for patients and visitors.

The skilful use of colour can help to overcome the sensory deprivation caused by lack of visual stimuli associated with drab or monotonous environments. Older people, long-stay patients and people with mental health problems have particular needs here (see sub-section 'Patients and visitors' in section 1.2).

Some hospital patients can go through emotional upheavals, which makes them more sensitive, and at the same time more receptive, to the emotional stimuli of colour and lighting. Patients with mental health problems have a particularly emotional experience and their reactions to colour have been shown to be extreme [1.7].

While colour does not in itself act as a cure, it does affect mood [1.8]; thus, the right colours can help to create a attitude which is therapeutic in the sense that it inspires confidence and can banish fear. The quest for the "correct" colour, however, is not as important as devising a scheme which enhances the building, whatever age it is, and thereby creates a harmonious environment.

Colour does, of course, also have a practical and functional use in patients' accommodation. Used with subtlety in all environments, it can be used to control reflected light, to make the most of available daylight and to help reduce glare. Used with strength, it can also be used for coding and identification purposes.

Lighting design should consider both daylighting and electric lighting. Both have important roles to play in providing appropriate visual conditions in terms of visual function and visual amenity. Visual function deals with the ability of the occupants to carry out their tasks efficiently. This not only includes the staff but also the patients and their visitors. Visual amenity refers to the creation of a lit environment that is appropriate for its purpose – to help the occupants feel comfortable, the staff to feel stimulated and the patients to feel confident and relaxed. The composition of surface colours will help with this visual impression; colour has both an aesthetic and practical function in changing the appearance of spaces [1.9]. Consideration of the interaction between light and surface colour and surface reflectance also needs careful examination (see sub-section 'Blankets and top linen' in section 2.4). Experiments have shown that a quantity termed "visual lightness" is positively correlated with occupant satisfaction [1.10].

High reflectance materials are required to give visual lightness, otherwise the surface – and hence the space itself – is likely to appear dark, even when high levels of light are used. Equally, limited areas of strong colour, such as those sometimes used in murals for children's wards, will need to be well-lit for them to have the full sense of vibrancy and to maintain interest after twilight. Lighting of such complex coloured designs needs to maintain a consistent appearance from day to night.

The architectural integration of the colour scheme and the lighting installation, including the equipment and the light pattern it provides, is another important aspect of design often overlooked [1.11]. Without awareness of these issues, there could be visual confusion and discord. The lighting and colour design needs to grow naturally from the architecture and the building use, and consultation between the various members of the design team is essential. The inherent colour of the construction materials used for the fabric of the building can form the first element in the planning and creation of a building's interior colour palette.

A lighting installation needs to be effective not only in human terms but also in terms of its energy efficiency. This will optimise the electricity used for lighting, which will have benefits in terms of hospital running costs as well as the wider implications of global warming. This stresses the need to balance capital costs against running costs to ensure the best through-life cost solution. Low capital costs can often lead to high running costs which over the life of the installation is an economy that can quickly be eroded. In this area, the designer will need to consider the equipment used, how the design is organised with respect to natural light, its use and how lighting is to be controlled both manually and automatically. It will also be necessary to comply with the Building Regulations Part L2 2000 [1.12].

Maintenance is another important area that needs to be considered at the design stage to ensure that both colour design and lighting are at a premium throughout the life of the facility. Damaged and dirty paintwork or dirty light fittings and failed lamps suggest poor housekeeping and can give out the wrong message to visitors, patients and staff.

A poorly maintained lighting or colour scheme will also waste money through wasted energy when the lighting loses its effectiveness. It will also affect users' perceived level of confidence in the efficiency of the environment.

This publication deals with colour (Chapter 2) and lighting (Chapter 3) in more detail, and provides specific guidance for the range of situations and applications covered by this guide in Chapter 4.

1.2 Hospital users

Hospital design needs to reflect the wide range of their users, whether patients, visitors or staff.

Patients and visitors

For patients and visitors, entering a hospital is often a stressful and uncertain time. To meet their needs, the NHS strategy has been to provide flexibility in services and to adopt a patient-oriented attitude towards improving the hospital environment.

A UK study on improvements in patient recovery [1.4] found that patients were released one-and-a-half days earlier in a refurbished environment compared with an unchanged one, and time spent in an intensive supervisory care area in a mental health unit was reduced by 70%.

A USA research project [1.13] established eight consistent themes in what patients and their families look for in the hospital's built environment. They wanted an environment that:

- facilitates connection to staff;

- facilitates connection to the outside world. This included an indoor environment that revealed sights and scenes from nature (see Figure 1.1);

- is conducive to a sense of well-being; that is "homely" (particularly in long-term care), "attractive", "inviting", "cheerful", relaxing, with positive distractions in waiting areas and an environment that facilitates autonomy and independence;

- is convenient and accessible – clear signs, visual clues and easy wayfinding were important;

- promotes confidentiality and privacy;

- is caring of the family;

- is considerate of impairments – long corridors, lack of seating, inappropriate signage are cited as problems;

- is safe and secure.

For patients and visitors, colour and lighting design can bring a welcome distraction from the problems that have resulted in hospitalisation. This can be accomplished with a careful selection of details such as décor, landmarks, artwork, the skills of interior landscape gardening and window designs (see Figures 1.2 and 1.3). In one hospital, an aerial photograph of the area is used on the ceiling of an examination and treatment area, which is a particularly stressful environment. Patients become absorbed searching for their home in the photograph.

Older people and the visually impaired

Older people form an important and growing subset of the hospital population. They are more likely to need several treatments and to stay in hospital for longer periods (on average one-to-three weeks). They have particular visual and non-visual requirements that make good lighting and colour design important.

Figure 1.1 A window, view out or internal view onto a courtyard is a vital link to the outside world

Figure 1.2 Patients find landmarks and décor a welcome distraction. They can also aid orientation and wayfinding

Figure 1.3 Courtyard and landscape gardening can provide visual interest in an urban or suburban context

As a person's visual system ages, various changes become apparent [1.14, 1.15]:

- The eye finds it harder to focus at close range. Older people usually require reading glasses or varifocal lenses for close work.

- The retina receives less light because of increasing lens absorption and reduced pupil size. It is estimated that, for the same light level, a 60-year-old receives about one-third the retinal illuminance of what a 20-year-old receives. It is recommended that [1.14] "at least three times more light will be needed in task areas to see fine details".

- More light is scattered within the eye. This has two impacts: (1) the contrast of the image on the retina decreases, making it harder to see; (2) the scattered light also decreases the vividness of colours.

- Because of yellowing in the lens, older people become less sensitive to wavelengths of light at the blue end of the spectrum.

- The eye becomes slower to adapt between bright and dim conditions. Travelling from dim to bright appears to be the most disabling [1.16] (see Figure 1.4).

Figure 1.4 Adaptation between extremely different lighting conditions is slower as a person's visual system ages. Lighting design should provide well-lit transition areas to accommodate moving from dim to brightly-lit areas

Older people are more likely to have some more serious form of visual defect. Other users of hospitals may also have difficulty seeing. They do not have to be registered blind or visually impaired people, but could be people who have forgotten their correction equipment (glasses, etc) or people who have temporary impairment due to an illness, stress or a treatment (for example, migraine headaches).

A person's type of visual impairment and their visual acuity determine what they can see. Only 4% of registered blind people have no sight at all. Many are able to make out shapes and contrasts in colour [1.17]. People with cataracts are more likely to have problems with glare (Figure 1.5) and a reduction in the ability to see short wavelengths (blues), while long wavelengths (yellows, oranges) are accentuated [1.18]. For difficult visual tasks, a cooler colour of light may be preferred (see sub-section 'Task illumination' in section 3.2). Tritanopia (total colour-blindness) is frequently observed in diabetic retinopathy [1.18]. This obviously has implications for the colour design of signage (see sub-section 'Signage' in section 2.3).

Figure 1.5 Strong lights shining from back-illuminated signage can cause glare problems for people with cataracts

Visually impaired and older people like to feel comfortable and in control. Feeling in control includes knowing where they are and where they are going [1.19]. People with low vision concentrate on looking at floors or at waist level at walls. They use the ceiling for spatial perception and orientation, skirting-floor and skirting-wall junction for assistance, and door handles and frames for identifying doors [1.19] (Figure 1.6). Visually impaired people feel more confident if they can identify the location of doors [1.18]. Strong contrast between objects and obstacles as well as text in signage (Figure 1.7) is required. The use of colour for wayfinding or orientation (section 2.3) should be boosted by careful illumination to provide adequate guidance and safety [1.19].

Other disabled people

Other categories of disabled people [1.20] have special requirements for sensitive lighting and colour design:

- Wheelchair users need lighting on low level controls. Signage should be clearly lit when viewed from wheelchair level. Places where people

Figure 1.6 Use of strong contrast on potential obstacles, such as edges of doors, aids safety and accessibility for all

transfer to or from a wheelchair may need extra lighting. The positions of glazed surfaces should be checked for adverse reflections and glare. These may occur where pictures and windows are at the wrong angle or level for wheelchair users and not obvious to the fully mobile.

- Lighting of reception desks should be positioned so that the receptionist's face can be clearly seen by people with hearing impairment who can lip-read. Standard mains frequency lighting can cause a hum in hearing aids. High frequency electronic ballasts will cure this problem.

- Confined environments, and those with certain strong colours, can be threatening spaces to those with mental health problems. Lighting and colour should make these spaces seem as bright and open as possible (see section 5.1) [1.21]. In interviews, 45% of patients [1.22] with mental health problems said ward conditions had a negative effect on their health. Some of them also stated that they had an intolerance of oranges and reds.

The use of such colours to "cheer up" an environment is not always appreciated by the patients and can produce over-stimulation [1.7].

Authorities are reminded of the need to comply with the provisions of:

- the Disability Discrimination Act 1995 (updated 2001) [1.23];

- BS 8300: 2001 'Design of buildings and their approaches to meet the needs of disabled people. Code of practice' [1.24];

- the Building Regulations. Approved Document M: Access and facilities for disabled people, 1999 [1.25];

- the Disabled Persons (Services, Consultation and Representation) Act 1986 (updated 2000) [1.26].

Young patients

The very young also have particular requirements from a lighting and colour design scheme. New-born babies, especially those born prematurely, are particularly susceptible to bright light, which can cause stress [1.6] and also retinal damage [1.27]. They need a recognisable pattern of night and day, however, to help them develop diurnal rhythms and normal sleep patterns [1.28]. Older children may find a hospital stay stressful. Good colour design can make the hospital appear less institutional and a more pleasant and stimulating place to be in.

Scale and perspective are crucial to understanding the design of environments for children [1.29]. Some external entrances are child-centred in scale and of sufficient visual stimulation internally to distract a child for a while (Figure 1.8). Very young children are much more aware of colour and shape than form (Figure 1.9). They use touch much more than adults, exploring floors and surfaces with their hands. Children, both patients and visitors, can find hospital environments boring and fearful; colour design can help them by providing visual interest and an emotional outlet. Some excellent examples are given in the NHS Design Portfolio [1.30].

One group that needs a special approach is the adolescent in hospital; it has been difficult to cater for this age group as neither adult nor child spaces are entirely appropriate. The younger person has a definite viewpoint on what constitutes an acceptable environment (Figure 1.10).

Figure 1.7 Text should always contrast with backgrounds to achieve maximum perception, especially where used for signage to be seen from a distance

Figure 1.8 An external entrance to a children's unit is scaled down for a child's perspective. External illumination has been reduced in height

Figure 1.9 Children explore and "use" floors and find colour and shape more important than form. They use touch to explore and investigate, which helps to divert their attention, whether they be patient or visitor

Special units have been successfully developed to allow this age group to develop and customise their own environment in much the same way as they might do in their own homes [1.31].

Staff

Good colour and lighting design in hospitals can facilitate the work of the staff and even make their work easier, practically, psychologically and emotionally.

Staff often have clear views on the design and definition of their workplace. Many NHS trust establishments involve staff in the design and development of their workstations for example (Figure 1.11). This can include everything from suggestions for artwork and small improvements to major refurbishment decisions.

During the audits and surveys undertaken, staff in various establishments stated that they required an environment which ensured:

- recruitment and retention of staff;
- improved morale;
- accessibility and orientation;
- privacy and security.

The King's Fund's [1.32] clinically led programme of environmental improvements over some 43 NHS trusts within the London area received a positive response in our surveys with nursing staff. Design schemes are developed with design consultants and training provided by paint and lighting manufacturers. Staff interest and involvement have led to some successful results, with an improved atmosphere (Figure 1.11).

In some children's wards, the staff have had considerable input into the look of the ward. In one hospital, a number of small rooms were decorated without a specific theme so that they looked like "homely bedrooms", and staff encouraged the parents to bring in personal items from home (Figure 1.12).

Staff require a space for privacy, time out and contrast from the workstation. The provision of a user-friendly workstation is an important place where they can deal with all the many tasks involved and also see and be seen by patients. (Figure 1.13). Colour design and lighting can make the staff's job a lot easier by providing the best possible viewing conditions, making it approachable for all users of the building.

Vision is at its best when there is ample light on the task [1.33] and when a number of conditions are fulfilled:

- The overall surround must be neither too bright nor too dim.
- Glare sources, whether direct or indirect, are eliminated.
- Walls and floors should have a reasonable range of brightness levels.
- Excessive contrast is not visible in the immediate background to any task.

Insufficient illumination, glare or excessive differences of brightness within the field of view can cause considerable discomfort to those who have to

Figure 1.10 A waiting room designed by a 19 year old showing their priority for key features

Figure 1.11 Staff developed this scheme of a refurbishment at an Endoscopy Unit. It improved the working environment for tasks (above) and improved the atmosphere welcoming people to the unit (below)

Figure 1.12 Parents were encouraged to bring in personal items from home to "customise" a children's ward

perform a task which requires visual concentration (Figure 1.14). The muscles of the eye, which regulate the pupil opening and which are responsible for accommodation and convergence of the eye, become tired and fatigued [1.3]. Although the eye is highly durable, it is an organ that can easily become strained by adverse conditions.

Figure 1.13 The staff workstation is important for regular staff, visiting staff, patients and visitors. It should always be approachable by everyone, especially wheelchair users

Figure 1.14 Nurse workstation lighting should be balanced and not extremely contrasting with other illuminance levels in the immediate vicinity

2. Colour design and interiors

2.1 Colour design

Colour design for interiors covers all materials and surfaces, including everything from light and paint to art and ambience, from aesthetics to functionality. It is an inherent property of materials and an inseparable component of design. Colour design can play a part in the healing process and add to a sense of well-being [2.1].

This section of the guide will provide some methods for arriving at final colour design schemes. These range from clinical guidance on colours for areas dealing with specific medical conditions to the colour measurement of existing paint colours to be retained in a refurbishment project and incorporated into a new scheme. However, decisions about the colours used in an environment will always remain for many people a personal or subjective issue. Sometimes, however, individual preferences have seen the creation of unpleasant solutions to particular environments, which could have been avoided with some basic knowledge about the way in which colour behaves.

Unfortunately, there is no simple prescription for preparing a colour design specification. Colour design can be included in design schemes for all areas: from the material colours of the building exterior and its approaches to the patient's bedside (Figure 2.0).

This guidance presents some fundamental issues to help those developing colour schemes to satisfy the majority. It is useful at this stage to point out "what not to do" or "what not to leave out" when thinking through some strategies for creating colour design schemes.

In healthcare environments, cost, maintenance and the storage of paint materials are important issues related to colour. Sometimes this can lead to a single colour dominating the environment, such as magnolia [2.2], with a heavy institutional feel found in many of the older establishments that have not been refurbished. Two tones of a colour can help if variety of colour is restricted (Figure 2.1).

Creative colour schemes can lead to more stimulating environments, which will be of benefit to all users. The promotion of a greater sense of well-being, particularly in long-term-care environments, is also possible if the colour scheme is carefully planned. This need not increase the cost or difficulty of maintenance substantially.

In all hospital areas, where appropriate, some basic colour design guidance should be:

- **Use tonal contrast:** to provide a difference between adjacent surfaces to enhance visibility for users, especially the elderly or visually impaired (Figure 2.2).

Figure 2.0 Colour design should be considered in all schemes from the exterior approaches to the building (top) to the patient's bedside (above)

Figure 2.1 A single colour scheme can create a monotonous environment – but using two tones of a colour can create some visual interest

- **Provide tonal detail:** to differentiate architraves, door frames, skirting and doors from their immediate surroundings by the use of depth (for example, raised mouldings to give shadow detail);

- **Preserve existing/historical features** of the building that enhance its designed form. Appropriate materials and features which are of value in terms of the building's architectural form should be incorporated into the colour palette instead of being altered to fit in with colour schemes (see sub-section 'Architectural integration' in section 3.2).

- **Limit the colour palette** when choosing internal finish materials, using a lot of differing colours may lead to an environment which is too visually busy, leading to confusion and unease (Figure 2.3). It may also cause maintenance and storage problems of materials for repair (see section 2.4).

- **Coordinate colours** of the building and existing finishes with paint for colour harmony (see sub-section 'Colour harmony' in section 2.2). If appropriate and possible, try to coordinate colours of materials such as flooring with other finishing materials used. For example, the colour reference of the floor material could be given to a textile manufacturer to be incorporated in colourways for curtain designs (see sub-section 'Colour referencing' in section 2.2).

- **Provide continual visual interest with a variety of colour and lighting levels:** this will ensure that users do not have feelings of boredom or under-stimulation due to monotonous visual environments.

- **Use colour and contrast** in materials and textures to create surfaces which are tactile, visually stimulating and which use lighting to maximise shadow detail (Figure 2.4).

Figure 2.2 Use of contrast and tonal detail for accessibility is provided by a colour design guidance strategy

Figure 2.3 Limiting the colour palette to reduce visually busy environments such as wards

Colour design and contrast for the visually impaired and older people

Some people have impaired vision for a variety of short or long-term reasons. A relatively small percentage of people have no vision at all, so using colour and contrast may enhance the environment considerably for this group of users. Many visually impaired people can make out a certain level of contrast in everyday lighting conditions, so it is useful, for example, for walls and floors to be of different light reflectances.

Contrast does not necessarily have to be black and white. As a general rule, a 20–30% difference in light reflectance value is sufficient for most people to understand environments more easily. For further information on colour or contrast for visually impaired people, refer to Bright et al [2.3] or advice and guidance on design from CDRG [2.4].

Colour and contrast are the most economical and effective tools for designing functional environments that are easy to use. Using colour contrast can be beneficial in helping visually impaired and elderly users to understand the spatial orientation of surfaces such as stairs, floors or doors.

Some design applications that can aid visually impaired people and the elderly are given below. Since nearly all areas of a hospital will have visually

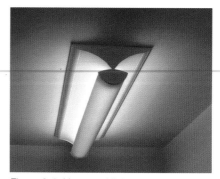

Figure 2.4 Use good lighting to maximise shadow detail on walls and ceilings

impaired or elderly visitors, the following points represent good practice in almost every situation [2.3].

- Wall colour should be sufficiently different from ceiling, floor and door colours.

- Stair nosings (the edge of the front and top of the step) should be in a solid colour to contrast with the stair tread (see sub-section 'Stairs and escalators' in section 4.3).

- Door handles, finger-plates and kick boards should be of stainless steel, or be significantly different in colour from the door itself (Figure 2.5).

- Vertical edges of doors should contrast in colour from the rest of the door – open doors can be very hazardous for the visually impaired (see Figure 1.6).

- Switches, controls and buttons of any kind should contrast with walls and hardware (for example, see sub-section 'Lifts' in section 4.3);

- Potential obstacles and free-standing objects should be coloured in such a way that they stand out from their surroundings (Figure 2.6).

- There should be a strong contrast between the floor planes and features that extend from ground level, such as signage, columns, telephone booths and literature displays (for example, see sub-section 'Toilets' in section 4.2).

- Visually mark changes in floor gradients or slopes with colour and contrast to alert people.

- There should be strong colour-contrast areas at the approaches to tops and bottoms of stairs and escalators.

- The side-panels of a staircase well should contrast with the treads to produce a zigzag pattern to aid users descending or ascending stairs.

- Limit usage of reflective (mirror-like) surfaces, as they might be detrimental for navigating.

- Use matt floor finishes to aid navigation and reduce reflections and glare from downlighters or windows (Figure 2.7).

- Distinguish skirting/floor and skirting/wall junctions with contrasting colours for assistance in navigation.

- Handrails which contrast with walls and are attached to a wall at waist height are a good aid. They should be applied to all staircases and could be considered in wards for older people.

The colour-design audit

Carrying out a colour-design audit on-site, whether the building be new or existing, is the first stage in developing a colour scheme for an interior.

For refurbishments, this type of site audit provides essential information and is of critical importance for reasons of conservation and to retain some continuity, harmony or unity. In a colour-design audit, all features which have to be retained can be measured, plotted or referenced (see sub-section 'Colour referencing' in section 2.2). This may include anything from the shade of white on some historic architectural or decorative detail to the inclusion of the colour of ducting panels that cannot be camouflaged but which could be incorporated somehow into the colour scheme. The audit

Figure 2.5 All door furniture should contrast sufficiently from the door itself

Figure 2.6 Potential obstacles such as seating which might be dangerous should be finished in contrasting colours

Figure 2.7 Reflections on glossy floors cause disturbing glare and lack of confidence for older and visually impaired people

should include observation of any details such as general traffic areas, existing lighting conditions, the retention of existing details such as Terrazzo floor tiling, plaster ceilings or even stained-glass windows. (Figures 2.8 and 2.9)

Colour-design site audits carried out by colour consultants would involve at least one form of colour referencing and should include colour measurement of existing surfaces in situ. Once the data (of the existing material colours) has been established and plotted in colour space, the strategy for a new scheme can be constructed (Figure 2.10).

If the site is to be newly built, the task is made more challenging by the need to fully understand the architectural drawings. These will indicate the orientation of the building and any obstructions affecting potential daylight illumination levels. Details of the areas which each user of the building might visit in a single day during a long-term stay or visit are all essential to planning a successful colour scheme.

The colour scheme

There can be no set formulae for colour schemes. As already mentioned, the context, existing materials and, of course, the locality will have a big influence on what designers would use as a starting point for a colour scheme. This check-list, though, should make a useful starting point:

- Carry out a site audit, external and internal, for new build and refurbishment, including orientation of the building, proximity of other sites etc.

- Plot all colours of existing materials and retained surfaces, for example, flooring, marble steps (Figures 2.9 and 2.10).

- Identify all accessibility issues inherent in the spatial layout of the site where colour could be used. Look for areas where contrast is required and where it could improve the environment for all users of the building.

- Define the colour-coding and zoning issues which may affect the scheme. The new scheme may want to take advantage of some coding or zoning strategy.

- Evaluate the levels of natural light available and look at quality of artificial illuminance. This may affect, for example, which wall can be safely coloured in a brighter shade. You may need light reflecting off a light wall or you may wish to light up a particularly bright colour in a dark area of a corridor with little or no natural light (Figure 2.11).

- Analyse colours to be used (for example, existing or proposed) to arrive at a key light or pastel colour to be used throughout the site. This may be crucial in integrating a site that has many additional units tacked onto a main building. Do not rule white out if you are planning to use many colours. A typical problem is that white is seen as hygienic and clinical, so is sometimes desired by users [2.5]. However, evidence does suggest that an all-white environment can cause visual under-stimulation and therefore stress for long-term-stay patients. "Neutral environments produce anything but neutral effects" [2.6].

- Plan a consistent scheme, which acknowledges everything from the aesthetic detail of the architecture to the clinical needs of staff. Colour may be derived from existing marble or plaster work or, for example,

Figure 2.8 An audit should include all the information about every historical and architectural detail to ensure integration of the scheme with the preservation of the building's character

Figure 2.9 Include colours of existing materials in plans for a refurbishment scheme, for example Terrazzo flooring

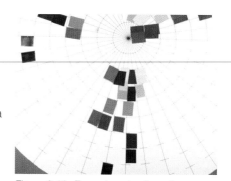

Figure 2.10 Examples of colours from a site audit, referenced and organised to analyse existing material colours of the site: e.g. powder-coated railings, brickwork, stone paving and wall colours

from a need to avoid yellow in an area where the the skin tone of new-borns is checked for jaundice.

- Interpret colour psychology theories for use within hospital environments with caution and avoid major personal colour preferences at first.

- Identify the specific ambient requirements of areas: for example, reception, corridors, waiting rooms, wards, nurses' stations, dayrooms, children's entrance etc.

- For each area, use a limited palette of colours. A large percentage of 80% of a paler colour is advisable. These colours could be opposite harmonic colours such as blue and yellow (Figure 2.12) (see also sub-section 'Colour harmony' in section 2.2). Darker tones of these two colours could be used in flooring or architrave detail or contrasting doors or handles.

- You may want the scheme to "tell a story" such as a waterfall which moves through levels of a building with sequences of colours and imagery. For this, a range of four distinct colours spanning the blue/green adjacent colours could be used (see sub-section 'Colour harmony' in section 2.2).

- Use colour in corridors to signpost a ward with a steadily decreasing level of chroma (or strength of colour) as you move towards the ward and bed area (Figure 2.13).

- Keep the number of colours to a minimum so that repair work can be carried out satisfactorily in the future.

- Note that colours which are greyed-off or toned down are relaxing and recede visually. This has been found to be very calming.

- Never choose or select a colour from a small patch. Apply a large area of a test pot of paint to a wall or paint the inside of a large cardboard box.

Finally, some general advice on colours. Colours which have not been recommended by designers in the past have been strong dark blues which can be very cold; yellow/greens because they can be associated with nausea; purple mainly due to superstition or prejudice associated with the colour; and brilliant reds for clinical reasons. Neutral colours such as beige, grey and cream can be very functional and useful colours for interiors. They are soft and can provide a warm effect, free of sharpness and also moderately stimulating. A tint of a beige wall colour can be used for ceilings. With inexperienced teams, developing colour schemes the use of neutral colours can be used and be accented with other colours and devices.

2.2 Colour fundamentals

Colour and light

Colour serves to control and reflect light. Ceilings and floors as well as walls are particularly important as reflectors of light and should be finished in light colours over most of their area if possible. Even the surrounding ground outside a building can reflect light into windows (Figure 2.14). Using light surfaces around the exterior of a building, such as light walkways, deep but

Figure 2.11 A more imaginative artificial lighting scheme is required for strong coloured dark wall areas as in this corridor scheme

Figure 2.12 Two opposite harmonic colours are used to create a visually stimulating colour scheme for a dayroom

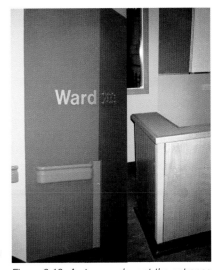

Figure 2.13 A strong colour at the entrance to the ward off a main corridor (left) is used in decreasing strengths in stages towards the nurse workstation (right) then further on to a pale pastel colour in the ward bedside area

light painted reveals around the window or light window sills all help to boost light levels entering the building.

In turn, lighting has a considerable bearing on choice of colour. In large wards, the lighting and colour scheme will need to be carefully designed to provide the right ambience at the back of the room away from any windows. Small windows may require brighter window walls to relieve the contrast of a small bright window seen against a dark solid wall (Figure 2.15). This can be achieved with a combination of lighting and colour.

The relative appearance of surface colours can change depending on the type of light under which they are seen (see 'Colour matching' sub-section below). Areas of a hospital are often daylit but at night time need to be illuminated by artificial light (Figure 2.16). A balance is required between providing good colour rendering of people's faces and good colour definition generally, and producing an adequate upbeat light environment to sustain the daytime ambience into night-time.

Colour matching

Colour of objects and surfaces can behave unexpectedly under varying lighting conditions. When setting up a colour scheme and choosing materials, it is important to view all the material samples underneath the types of light sources that will be used within the hospital itself. In a daylit space this will involve matching and comparing colours under daylight as well as under the colour of fluorescent lighting that will be used. The light source with which a coloured surface is illuminated can affect its colour appearance. It is possible for a pair of coloured materials which match under one light source (for example daylight) to look totally different under another source, such as fluorescent light.

This can happen if the two materials are coated or dyed with colours that were not derived from the same pigments. They can behave differently under the alternative light source and not match. This is known as metamerism. Metamerism occurs when spectral curves of the two samples cross more than twice if overlaid. Measuring coloured surfaces with a spectrophotometer (see sub-section 'Colour referencing' below) can predict such mismatches without actually having to observe the samples under different illuminants.

One further complication to using colour under different lighting sources is colour constancy. When people observe a space, the colour relationship between all the colours of the features in view appears to remain stable even when the illuminant is changed, unless the lighting has poor colour rendering (see section 3.2). The eye largely compensates for illuminant changes. Therefore people do not see dramatic colour changes when the type of lighting changes. For example, reds will still look red compared with other colours, although specific red colours may no longer look red if photographed for example; our eyes adjust to the shift of colours under these different sources.

Figure 2.14 Light-coloured aggregate or paving material on surrounding pathways can enhance levels of reflected light back into the building interior

Figure 2.15 Dark window walls should be light in colour and tone and have some directional lighting on them to alleviate stark contrast. Bright daylight entering the room, without wall washers, can make these walls appear gloomy

Figure 2.16 Evening or night-time illumination needs to preserve the consistency of ambience from daytime into the evening

Colour backgrounds and skin tone

The effects on perception of skin-tone colour caused by the colour of backgrounds and the colour-rendering qualities of the light source are important for two main reasons (Figure 2.17). First, the ambience of a building is often judged from how our faces and others' appear in the given lighting conditions against given background colours. It has been suggested that convalescing patients should be given warm-coloured lamps, which are generally flattering to most skin tones, improving the appearance of the patient and their sense of optimism and well-being.

However, the complex combinations of environmental colour, skin-tone or colour of pigmentation and lighting in the clinical environment are also important for diagnosis.

The identification of medical conditions by appraisal of changes in skin-tone is an everyday practice for nurses and a major part of a medical examination for many conditions. Dermatology, for example, would rely heavily on the assessment of visual appearance of skin for diagnosis. In this field, special colour schemes approved clinically should be implemented to allow for diagnosis and treatment to be carried out in the optimum environment, that is careful lighting and neutral backgrounds.

Lamps with a "very good" or "excellent" colour-rendering index (section 3.2) are needed so that the skin colour can be checked [2.5]. One comment from staff suggested that more nursing staff training is required on this area of skin tone, health and skin pigmentation.

The wide range of patients' skin tones and pigmentation is certainly a challenge to finding the ideal coloured background for wards or walls behind patients' beds, not forgetting the inclusion of colour reflections from surroundings (Figure 2.18). Many visits to patients' bedsides occur after lunch, when patients may be resting in subdued light. The best colour background for judging colour and colour change is grey, which is not an ideal colour to decorate a ward. However, "greyed" décor colours that contain a small proportion of black are useful on two counts:

- The colour contains the necessary element of neutrality, a grey.

- Greyed colours are known to be very relaxing and stress-reducing [2.7].

Greyed colour may not be ideal in, for example, a children's area or a maternity unit where people may expect to be in a more upbeat environment. To demonstrate the importance of an awareness of how colour perception can be dramatically affected by colour surround and lighting, Figure 2.19 shows the problems that can arise in appraisal of skin tone. Reflected colour, for example, from blinds and curtains can also affect the appearance of surfaces and surroundings in a clinical situation (see sub-section 'Blankets and top linen' in section 2.4).

Colour referencing

A successful colour design strategy for an environment is based, first, on a combination of balancing colour requirements with an understanding of the different types of light source. After that, many colour schemes involve concepts of "harmony" or "adjacency" or "opponent" colour theory; the

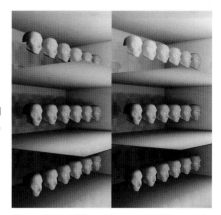

Figure 2.17 Different types of lighting such as fluorescent (left) or incandescent (right) renders skin-tone appearance differently, from flattering to unhealthy. Each row is made of different skin-tones shown in front of different tonal backgrounds and light sources demonstrating results on appearance

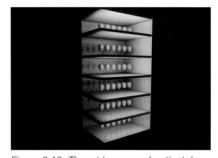

Figure 2.18 The wide range of patients' skin tones and pigmentation is certainly a challenge to finding the ideal coloured background for clinical appraisal

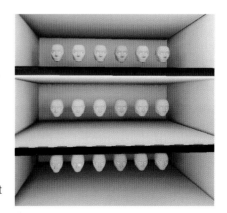

Figure 2.19 Each row of faces made up of different skin tones is the same. Only background colour and lighting have changed for each row

structure of a colour reference system can provide a useful strategy or framework on which to build.

There are many types of colour referencing systems in use today (for example, NCS, Pantone, Dulux Colour Palette, British Standards and RAL). Most are systems that have been developed for commercial or industrial purposes and are driven by specific industrial needs. Some systems were developed for use originally in specific countries (Figure 2.20) [2.2].

Historically, British Standard colour references were developed to rationalise and coordinate the building trades' referencing of diverse materials including paints, coatings and building components. They are still in strong favour with many practices today. British Standard colour references for paint might be matched with colours for guttering or enamel coatings of cast-iron fencing. The system achieved some unity across a very broad range of construction materials.

The colour reference systems such as NCS that are used in industry (including the popular Munsell System) are in a sense artificial methods of organising and structuring colour. One approach to defining coloured surfaces that has established international agreement is the CIE Colour Space (CIELab) (Figures 2.21 and 2.22). CIELab is based on the colour measurement of a surface and places the colour as a three-dimensional reference point in colour space with an "L, a, b" reference.

Colour measurement is one way of establishing the existing material and surface-colour specifications found on a site. Measuring colour using the CIELab system is the nearest absolute currently available for identifying colour for repeatability, quality control or matching. Colour measurement equipment (a spectrophotometer or colorimeter) is expensive, ranging from £1000 to £12,000 depending on the degree of the task (Figure 2.23). A spectrophotometer can, however, plot the colour reference points of any material in colour space, and these can be conveyed to any second or third party to ensure a level of colour quality control or matching. A colour consultant would measure every component used in a new building or refurbishment and plot the results in colour space, providing the framework for creating a new colour design specification (Figure 2.9).

These components may be as diverse as powder-coated trunking, flooring or anodised aluminium window frames or existing historical details of a building. Hospital flooring in one colour scheme was used as a reference for the design and manufacture of the curtains, so the whole hospital palette was coordinated (Figure 2.24). Most manufacturers of materials and products for the built environment will provide on request colour references of materials such as paint. CIELab measurements offer the only "translation tool" for matching across different material surfaces. Difficult surfaces such as metallics, translucent or transparent materials are not easy to measure and require very specialised equipment.

Optical colour mixing

Optical colour mixing of patterns when viewed from afar can present a challenge to the interior designer. When selecting colourways of patterned materials such as curtain textiles, carpets or linoleum flooring, it should be borne in mind that a small design can appear very different when seen at a distance. The further away the pattern, the more that warmer colours in the design will dominate.

Figure 2.20 Examples of commercial colour reference systems

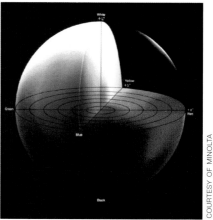

Figure 2.21 CIELab Colour Space 3D

COURTESY OF MINOLTA

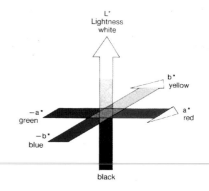

Figure 2.22 CIELab 3D Colour Space showing the poles L, a and b by which colour is plotted

Figure 2.23 An example of a commercial portable spectrophotometer for measuring colour

The optical mixing of colours is not as easy or logical as it might seem. For example, the effect of patterns in carpets observed from 25 metres away may bear no relation to the paint colours selected to match the patterned flooring. It is best to coordinate finishes, especially those with small patterns or designs, in situ and at the most likely viewing distances, including long distances where appropriate and with the same light source to be used in the location (Figure 2.25).

Colour preference

Colour preference is not simply a question of personal taste. There is some consensus on colour preferences among individual viewers and among experts [2.8].

In much published material on colour preferences worldwide, it has been found that blue is a continuously popular colour, regardless of culture, object, material or its presented medium. Thus, in laboratory environments, blue appears to be a preferred colour, while yellow is not [2.8–2.11].

It may be that blue is comfortable to the eye, thus being a safe choice, but there is at this point no firm evidence for this. Certainly blue's shorter wavelengths and low representation in cone sensitivity may contribute to blue being easy on the eye as opposed to yellow which uses all remaining potential cone sensitivity, for example red plus green. However, over-use of blue has been observed and may cause monotonous environments lacking variety, which would lead to boredom and under-stimulation (Figure 2.26). For guidance on this, see CDRG [2.4] and more information on colour preference and harmony studies see [2.8, 2.12, 2.13].

In hospital environments, a colour preference for "whiteness" or pale shades was found among patients with its connotations of cleanliness and hygiene [2.14]. Again caution should be taken not to over-use any single colour and to ensure a certain amount of variety in interiors to provide enough visual interest.

There are also colour preferences among staff for either practical or diagnostic reasons:

- In dermatology departments, orange is not recommended as a background colour. Staff in these units also reported that reds and oranges make patients feel itchy; yet orange was particularly popular for a maternity unit [1.10] (Figure 2.27).

- In cardiology, blue should not be used as it makes diagnosis more difficult.

- In maternity units, yellow should not be used as it hinders the diagnosis for jaundice.

- In mental health wards, oranges and reds are disliked.

- One hospital department suggested that green flooring was particularly good at showing up spills of body fluids, thus helping to prevent accidents due to slippery floors.

These points are only a few of the suggestions gathered from recent hospital audits.

Figure 2.24 Colour could be matched from the flooring and used for textile design to coordinate palettes

Figure 2.25 If possible view patterns (above) at a distance (top) to assess the potential optical mixture of the final colour in situ

Figure 2.26 Blue seems to be the favourite colour of many people worldwide regardless of culture, materials or objects, hence its use as a colour for hospital environments

Colour harmony

Harmonious colour schemes can be produced with a single hue such as blue, blue-green, red-blue or with a wide variety of colours, as long as there is some scheme for their selection.

Colour harmony is not based on personal taste; colour-harmony theories abound and have developed from analysis of colour circles, philosophers, artists' palettes and referencing colour over many centuries. They have also been adopted for interior colour schemes.

One approach to a harmonious colour scheme might be to use colour combinations in which the main hue remains the same but there are different versions of it (Figure 2.28). A single tonal scheme could include a deep blue for a door, a soft white with the same blue as a pale tint, and a flooring material which has a mid-saturation or chroma of the blue with dark and light flecks in linoleum. This would not be suitable for a long-term-stay ward where more variety would be required.

Alternatively, a scheme could use strong opposite colours in the colour circle, for example a dark blue used on doors and skirtings with a very pale yellow-orange on the walls (Figure 2.29). The relationship of the pale yellow-orange to the blue provides the harmonious link (opposite complementaries) (Figure 2.30).

Theories abound on how to choose harmonious combinations of colours according to their relative positions in colour space. A useful starting point is to choose two or three colours in a specified relationship to one another from a two-dimensional hue circle. These examples of relationships shown here between colours may be useful for building colour schemes using harmony (Figure 2.30) [2.15].

The fundamental colour harmony relationships are shown here in the left-hand column with their terminology whilst on the right are some suggestions made using those particular harmonies. They present variations of chroma or saturation as well as brightness or value (Figure 2.30).

Colour psychology

There is a considerable amount of published material, some empirical and much anecdotal, giving advice on colour application using theories of colour psychology. However, from experience it is suggested that this should not be followed indiscriminately. Contextual variables such as building materials used in construction, window positions or lighting, size of space, nearness of adjacent buildings or surface quality of materials can all dramatically affect colour appearance and behaviour of colour and override colour psychology recommendations (see sub-section 'The colour design audit' in section 2.1). These problems can be solved by a well-planned colour scheme which bases the colours selected for the building on a wide range of criteria which colour psychology theories cannot always cover. Some guidance is given below and in Chapter 4.

Recommendations on the usage of colour should also be applied carefully as over-use of a certain colour can cause problems. For example, overuse of green or blue colours, renowned for their calming effects, in mental healthcare environments may actually exacerbate depression (Figure 2.31) [2.16]. A priority should be that colour and lighting schemes should be

Figure 2.27 Orange was considered to be a suitably powerful and energetic colour for this maternity unit; successful here with a contrasting harmony of a purple in a connecting corridor

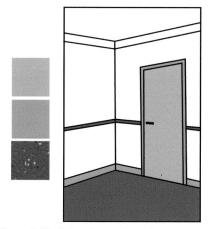

Figure 2.28 This colour scheme is a balance of a single hue, with variations in chroma (saturation) and brightness. A stronger version of the blue could be used for a short-stay unit such as a maternity department

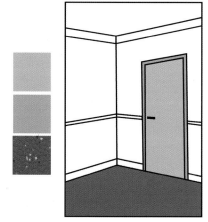

Figure 2.29 This colour scheme is a balance of two hues, blue and yellow-orange. The varying chroma and brightness of each creates a stimulating balance which could be used for a long-stay patient area for example

developed that enhance the building and create spaces where harmony is visible. The building itself needs ambience to affect the user's mood.

2.3 Colour design for navigation and signage

Colour is not only an aesthetic component of the environment, it can be a powerful navigation tool to help people find their way around a building (Figure 2.32). As colour can aid the memory in recalling shape and pattern, it is also a vital part of coding and signage if used correctly.

Navigation covers:

- **Orientation** – Provision of a sense of direction, course or point of reference.

- **Wayfinding** – Information to enable decision making and planning of routes.

- **Navigation** – Successful negotiation of the building and journey to a destination.

Signage covers:

- **Coding** – Provision of a visual system to simplify decision-making.

- **Zoning** – Division of a space into broad areas.

- **Signage** – Elements of the environment that provide information for users.

It is a mistake to develop wayfinding and signage in isolation and it should be included as an essential part of an integrated design scheme for the complete site if it is to be effective. Refurbishments and extensions need to fit in with this integrated scheme. The introduction of a new idea to an existing site, such as zoning, can lead to confusion unless it is carefully planned and implemented throughout the site from the car-park signs to the wards.

Orientation, wayfinding and navigation

People need to find their way in and around a hospital building that can be large and complex. It does not have to be confusing though. Good design of wayfinding elements can alleviate many of the major sources of frustration with negotiating environments [2.17]. To do this, people require well-designed, strategically placed levels of information to assist them at, what can be, a difficult and stressful time. Colour design can play a big part in helping people to find their bearings, to understand the spatial layout of the hospital, to note areas that have information about key routes on the site and to recognise that they have arrived at their desired destination.

Orientation

A good sense of orientation is a result of understanding a building's external form from the inside (Figure 2.33). Although the remit of this guide is the hospital environment from entrance and reception to ward, successful orientation commences as one enters a site from the main entrance to the site. Good plans, maps or models with simple colour-coding which emphasises the shape of the site are vital for spatial cognition, giving

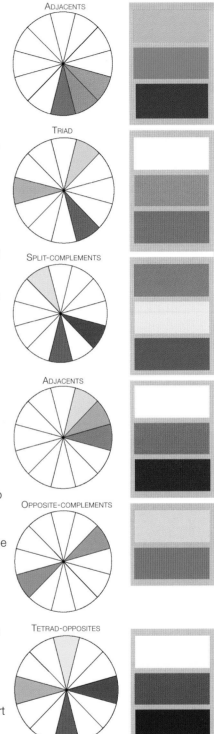

Figure 2.30 Colour harmony relationships (left) and examples of some possible colour schemes from those harmonies (right)

people the overall picture first. Views from the outside of key spaces, and views from circulation areas to the outside, help in the orientation process. Orientation employing colour for coding or zoning must be understood quickly and easily, from car-park directions for people entering the site in a car to the signage of different areas inside the hospital (Figure 2.34).

Wayfinding

Wayfinding is a decision-making and problem-solving process [2.18]. To provide information in the right way for users of a building is the goal of successful wayfinding. People need information to have confidence in making the right decisions about the right routes to take to avoid losing their way to a desired destination.

Comprehending the way spaces relate to one another and being able to see the underlying organisational principle of the circulation system are vital. Colour can simplify the graphical representation of site layouts, plans and charts, emphasising key routes, grouping areas and using colour-coding for simple zoning. The use of sculpture and other landmarks as mental anchors to provide unique points in space can be especially helpful in a wayfinding scheme [2.18] (Figure 2.35).

Understanding human behaviour is fundamental to establishing a fully practical system. Schemes have to work first time for the new user. Aiding independence is an aim of successful wayfinding schemes. A good approach is to ensure that wayfinding flows from the main circulation, source such as a lift lobby, with only as much information as is needed at each stage (Figure 2.36). Too much information often defeats successful wayfinding.

Navigation

Once a route is selected and users of the building have access to information or visual cues, they move around and through the building to their desired destination. This information gathering is a continuous process [2.18]. The consistency of the style of communication material (including colour, contrast and text) should not be tampered with; otherwise, the outcome of the scheme can be destroyed. All information must be repeated consistently and prioritised at specific crucial points in a building. In addition to the main reception desk, it is also important to provide information and assistance at central "one-stop shops". Finally, confirmation in wayfinding is often forgotten but vitally important to tell the person on a journey that they have finally arrived at their destination (Figure 2.37).

One vital requirement of a scheme is for wayfinding or signage managers to check whether it is successful in any direction and from any intersection, backwards and sideways throughout the building, day or night. However, the strategy should not produce an overload of visual information which can contribute to an already potentially stressful environment.

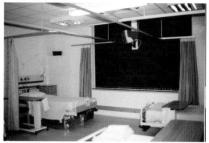
Figure 2.31 The overuse of certain blues and greens in mental healthcare environments may exacerbate depression

Figure 2.32 Colour can provide a sense of direction, a course or a strong asymmetrical reference point for spatial cognition, orientation and wayfinding

Figure 2.33 People, regardless of their language, can understand the general shape of the building from a good simple site map, essential for a sense of orientation when inside the building

Figure 2.34 Orientation employing colour for coding or zoning must be understood quickly and easily from entry to the site

Colour-coding

If orientation, wayfinding and navigation are the activities involved in using a building, coding, zoning and signage are the tools used to negotiate a building.

Colour-coding can be used to make sense of the environment and help simplify the site into wings, blocks and even internal "streets". Users of the building can differentiate between areas, departments and even buildings to get their bearings and find their way around [2.17]. Zoning, the definition of an area or section of the building by colour, is an important aspect of this.

Figure 2.35 Sculpture, artwork or other landmarks can act as powerful visual cues in a wayfinding scheme

Coding can be used in a range of ways. It can be included in site-maps and guides and then replicated in surface finishes. Walls and flooring can be in different colours in different departments. Alternatively, coded colours can be used to highlight, for example, skirtings, door frames, cornices and handrails.

One of the most important aspects of colour-coding is in the design of signage. But even in a simple building where coding is not needed, colour design still has an important impact on signage (Figure 2.38). This includes:

- **Clarity** – Use of optimum impact and legibility for communication

- **Contrast** – Ensuring all users can perceive objects and signs

- **Visual noise** – Ensuring that signs stand out from their surroundings and are not lost in, or contribute to, "clutter".

Figure 2.36 This lift-lobby area uses colour-coding which is also part of the navigation and floor-zoning system

Coding, zoning and signage are required at four stages in the journey through the hospital:

1 **Overall view** – At the beginning, to provide a sense of orientation in maps or guides to the site. This requires careful planning of the way in which colour will be used to convey spatial orientation.

2 **Support** – In signposting, to help the user make choices about directions; this must be both simple and informative without giving more information than is actually required at that point (Figure 2.39).

3 **Setting out** – Correctly placed or designed information to aid decision-making and confirmation of correct routes.

4 **Arrival at destination** – Details at the destination to verify reaching the target or goal (Figure 2.37).

Figure 2.37 Confirmation of arrival at the desired destination is important and often forgotten

Colour-coding can be an efficient method of assisting orientation as well as navigation within a building (Figure 2.40). However, coding is one of the most difficult applications of colour design in hospital environments and is not easy to retro-fit. It should ideally be kept very simple and is best implemented at the planning stage of a new building.

Colour-coding is often misunderstood by the people it is designed to help. Research has shown that it may not even be recognised by many users of environments. Two out of three people at healthcare sites that have a colour-coding system did not notice the colour-coding [2.17]. It is essential to identify why and for whom the colour-coding is being used.

If colour-coding is for patients and visitors, it should be easy to comprehend and should not be more than a few colours. If colour-coding is for hospital staff (for example, security staff, porters), more complicated

Figure 2.38 Colour used for cues in wayfinding is powerful. Information is required along the routes to enable decision-making and planning of routes

colour schemes could be used, provided that staff are briefed on the issue. In any case, it is strongly suggested that simple schemes be used to avoid confusion.

Over-enthusiastic colour-coding can dominate the environment. It is a tool and should not override the visual environment but it must be obvious (Figure 2.41). One way to limit the usage of colour, for example, is to apply it to only one wall of a corridor or to highlight door frames and skirting-wall and ceiling-wall junctions (see sub-section "Colour design and contrast for the visually impaired and elderly" in section 2.1). These highlights could be in different colours depending on the hospital department.

Placement of colour-coding or zoning needs to be well-considered (Figure 2.42). Being simple and consistent with the convention is vital so that people expect or anticipate the information they require. The best locations are at eye-level, on walls or lower down on the floor, since older or visually impaired people scan the floor and horizon and are more likely to use guidance below eye-level. Many hospitals have achieved success using basic coding on floors to provide boundaries or edges on walkways and routes (Figure 2.43). This is not easy to implement post-build as flooring is an expensive and relatively permanent material. Colour-coding and signage higher than eye-level or in a very cluttered or busy environment can often be missed.

Choosing the colour palette

Human eyes are exquisitely sensitive to colour variations; a colourist can distinguish among one million colours at least. For communicating abstract information, however, using more than 20 or 30 colours (tonal differences included) produces negative returns [2.19]. Where information coding in building signage is concerned, there is a need for an even more restricted range of four-to-five colours (Figure 2.44).

One approach is to choose from the rainbow colours of red, orange, yellow, green, blue, indigo and violet. The nature of the palette should encourage viewers to use colour names, which is helpful for identification and memory. In maintenance and refurbishment by estates departments, it is important for exactly the same colours to be used, otherwise people can become confused (for example, when a "blue-route" turns into a "turquoise-route") (Figure 2.47).

Where large areas of colour need to be used, pure, bright, very strong colours are less suitable; they may have loud, disharmonious effects when they are used over large areas adjacent to each other [2.19]. A few hospitals have used key colours below dado rails, which fulfils an accessibility, coding and wayfinding function (Figure 2.45). If used in a building that is of historical or architectural merit, colour schemes may have to be chosen and selected using a much wider range of criteria (see sub-section "Colour design" in section 2.1). It should be noted that strong colours may interfere with the lighting of a space reducing the potential for reflected light.

Around 8% of males and 1% of females have colour vision impairment. Usually this will affect the discrimination between red and green hues [2.17]. Certain visual impairments affect the ability to see differences between certain colours such as blue and green or even red and black. (see section 2.1) [2.20].

Figure 2.39 Signposting should be simple and informative to give people only the information that is actually required at that point

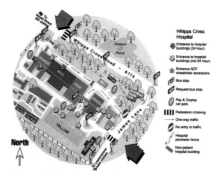

Figure 2.40 Simple colour-coding, if well-designed, can guide new visitors through an environment

Figure 2.41 Colour-coding should be obvious and easy for visitors to recognise and use. Care to avoid confusion with décor colours is essential

Figure 2.42 Too many colours converging in the environment can be confusing for coding and wayfinding

Colour and shape

Shape and colour are very successful partners in communication. They can help people remember information and can be used with other methods to build routes and pathways. Examples might be to adopt Green Square, Red Triangle or Blue Circle as a motif used in a coding system. Together, colour and shape motifs present few barriers except for some visually impaired people. Yellow usually presents problems in colour communication as it often has to be used with black text, where other colours would be using white text. It also is usually treated with outlining if used on a white background (Figure 2.46). This can be misconstrued and interrupt the consistency that is required for successful colour communication strategies.

Figure 2.43 Hospitals have implemented coloured wayfinding on floors but high contrast is required for people with low vision

Zoning

The use of colours and zoning is necessary if users of a building have little sense of orientation within the site. This may be due to the haphazard or "organic" growth of the hospital site (see section 5.4). Drawing together the disparate parts of a scattered site can be one of the main reasons for implementing a zone scheme.

However, attempts at zoning can compound the problems inherent in the spatial definition of the building and does not always resolve such problems that this kind of site presents to the designers. Thus the basis of the scheme should be as simple as possible, to make it easy for new visitors to the building, agency staff, visitors, young people and older people who all require easily accessible information.

The number of colours used for zoning should be kept to an absolute minimum. Colours used should have unique names such as Blue or Green and not Turquoise (Figure 2.47).

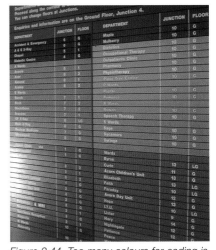

Figure 2.44 Too many colours for coding is not helpful for people new to a site. Keep the system simple to major zones

The following list should ideally be the largest number of colours used for zoning as a part of general orientation:

RED, ORANGE, YELLOW, GREEN, BLUE, PURPLE, PINK, BROWN, BLACK, WHITE, GREY [2.17].

Hospitals planning a new colour zoning strategy may have a variety of problems. For example, they may run out of significantly different colours or have to modify them afterwards. If red and orange were used, for example, as key colours, they might be inappropriate for a complete wall in a particular corridor, so lightening it to a pink and peach would be inconsistent and could cause confusion (Figure 2.48).

Signage

Signage is the tool to negotiate the environment and a key element of any wayfinding system [2.17]. However, simply putting up signs will rarely solve wayfinding problems. Ethnic diversity, especially in bigger cities, means that multiple languages are spoken by people using healthcare environments. One site was reported to be using 250 languages. The information they convey has to be accessible for all (Figure 2.49). Colour and lighting can be used to bring signage to the attention of users of the building and organise the hierarchy of information. However, in a survey of people using a hospital building it was found that as much as 80% of visitors rarely used signage but relied on other visual cues such as memorable features and landmarks.

Figure 2.45 Colour used for navigation on or below dado rails could be particularly useful for all users of the environment

Although highly functional, signage should also be well-designed and sufficiently visually acceptable not to detract from the environment.

Consistency is vital if a signage and colour scheme is to work. It helps people and gives them confidence. Local customisation, and even a change from lower case to capitals in signage, can cause confusion.

As most in-patients are in the building for an average of under three weeks, the patient population as a whole turns around at a considerable rate so a majority of people within the building are often new to the site. The challenge to the management of hospital environments is that most patients who enter the hospital expect to see logical and well-planned signage with guidance especially for them. Many people are visiting for the first time (Figure 2.50).

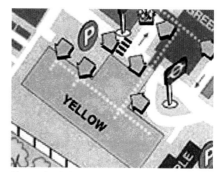

Figure 2.46 *Yellow used in coding with other colours generally has to be outlined in black and used with black text if on a white ground. This can create inconsistencies in signage and coding which often confuses people*

Clarity

Colour aids information to be clear and legible. Many of us recognise words as shapes, for example, EXIT, STOP or ENTRANCE, and colour helps people memorise these word-shapes, especially those people for whom English is not their first language (Figure 2.51). Textual, tactile or Braille information incorporated with well-designed pictograms is now widely used to assist in wayfinding using correct levels of contrast [2.17].

Figure 2.47 *The colours used in zones should have unique and particular names. Turquoise, for example, would be a problem if Blue and Green were used as well*

Rules and advice on the design of efficient signage are well documented. It has been shown in experiments in the USA [2.7] and Europe [2.21] that only certain colours maintain their visibility to the viewer at great distances. Orange retains its strength as a perceived hue longer than any other colour when placed at a great distance in daylight. Blue, however, was found to retain its strength over other colours as the light fades at twilight. Visually impaired people state that white text on a blue background is one of the most legible combinations for signage, as long as the text point size and typeface/font is strong, sans-serif and simple enough. Some people can have colour vision problems; 8% of males are colour-blind and some people with macular disease may see red as black. So any scheme for signage should have the colour visibility checked both indoors and outdoors for all types of vision.

Yellow is the only colour that is light in reflectance and at the same time intense and saturated enough to give a strong visual signal [2.19] (Figure 2.52). It is an appropriate hue for strong visual cues when used with black in hazard warnings. However, a visual aberration on the boundary lines between the black and yellow can cause dazzling and even physical pain in the eye for some visually impaired people, so this combination is surprisingly not always as popular as people have thought [2.22].

Figure 2.48 *Strong colours for zoning may look successful in two dimensions but are not so easy to translate to the built environment*

One other rule which is worth noting is that of scale and colour. The smaller the notice or object, the more important brightness and less relevant and easy to see is colour or hue. Some colours are difficult to perceive on a very small scale at a distance or outside. This would make certain colour-coding strategies unsuccessful. The reverse is also true that, for large signs or objects, hue or colour becomes more important (Figure 2.53).

On text, briefly legibility is assisted by simplicity. Ideal fonts are recommended by the RNIB [2.23]. Tiresias or Arial fonts that are sans-serif aid clarity of perception. Generous leading or line-spacing also helps text scanning (Figure 2.54).

Figure 2.49 *Easily accessible information for all is an essential aim of all signage, surmounting cognitive disability and language barriers*

Contrast

For people with low vision or visual impairment, signs, especially those needing to be seen and read from a great distance, should have a high level of contrast. Text requires at least a 60–70% difference in light reflectance values from background colour to achieve a reasonable chance of being read (Figure 2.54) [2.18]. But signage does not have to be as extreme as yellow on black to be functional. Some preliminary guidance exists already on this subject [2.17].

Visual noise

In hospitals, there is often a build-up of clutter or "visual noise" to which many of the staff become accustomed and it is a normal part of life in an environment (Figure 2.55). This level of visual noise may come from, for example:

- locally customised posters;

- the wide range of medical equipment in use or awaiting use where there is not enough storage space;

- badly situated or demarcated noticeboards; and

- inadequate control of signage design.

Clear space is one of the most important elements in being able to identify and perceive information quickly. Thus, if space is allotted and kept free around key information sites, then information can more easily be assimilated by everyone, with less visual distraction and stress (Figure 2.55). Ease of legibility can be more effectively guaranteed if clutter is kept to certain places only. Staff may be used to, or even unaware of, the high level of "visual noise" within the building, but it can lead to stress and confusion for everyone including the new visitor. Planning and managing places for communication or "clutter" can alleviate much of the stress caused by some visual noise where it is not wanted.

2.4 Colour and materials

Patients and staff all notice and appreciate a well-planned integrated colour scheme that includes all the various materials that can be used within the hospital environment from entrance to bed areas.

Steel and glass, used widely in modern buildings, create considerable problems especially for visually impaired people. Architects and designers have the challenge of resolving the impact of reflections, glare and the transparency of glass on the way users of the buildings interact with the environment. Manifestations can be decorative or functional.

Paint

Hospitals do not usually have enough space or money to accommodate large stocks of replacement materials; thus, it is good practice to rely on currently available lamps and paints (Figure 2.56). Maintenance issues are often raised when specifications select materials outside the list of normal products. For this reason, hospital facilities managers have in the past preferred to specify paint colours from British Standards. Although there is a

Figure 2.50 Logical and well-planned signage which is consistent reduces confusion while navigating the hospital environment

Figure 2.51 Colour can aid the clarity of information for all users of a building. Back-lit signage is very accessible for visually impaired people

Figure 2.52 Black and yellow are perfect for a contrasting colour combination. Other contrasting duos however can be used which have a less utilitarian appearance

Figure 2.53 The scale of text and symbols which need to be seen from a distance is important for legibility and colour contrast of all signage

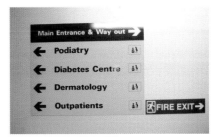

Figure 2.54 Contrasting, clear, well-organised text and arrows in signage help many people with low vision

limited range of available colours, which currently reflects past fashion trends in interiors more than today's preferences, they can use the code reference used by all paint manufacturers, which is convenient for any repair or repainting (Figure 2.57). It was reported that matching paint colours or convenience of supply was the main reason for specifying from a British Standard colour range. However, technology has moved on and most colours supplied by all the major manufacturers are easily repeatable and consistent in quality and match. There are also thousands of colours to choose from (see sub-section 'Colour referencing' in section 2.2).

Flooring

Carpets

When entering any environment a carpet achieves an immediate sense of quality and warmth underfoot (Figure 2.58). Carpets create an immediate impression within a reception area, although in this location they take the brunt of wear, weather and tear. Changes in texture of flooring help those people who require tactile information for guidance. Carpets also help acoustically, but they require high maintenance and have infection-control issues. They might need to be cleaned every night.

The carpet surface is not loved by wheelchair users or for anyone who has to push a trolley [2.24].

In NHS environments, carpets are usually only used in circulatory and reception areas where they receive considerable repeated all-weather use. High performance utility matting makes retention of water and moisture at thresholds possible. The opportunity for colour coordination of this type of matting or threshold with the continuing surface is not easy but could be more imaginatively developed by manufacturers. Possible provision of more comfort to the feet nearer bed areas, especially in long-term care areas, has been noted by some staff. Smaller versions of types of coloured-cotton, absorbent mats can be placed anywhere within a building where moisture may be a problem, are machine washable and can also be tumble-dried easily (Figure 2.59). The colour, texture and design of carpets and matting are difficult issues to get right. This is compounded by expense, durability as well as problems presented with maintenance and safety.

Many private hospitals have to use carpet throughout to convey a sense of luxury to both patients and visitors. However it has been impossible to guarantee that this type of flooring is always completely clean and hygienic [2.25].

Hard flooring

Hard flooring such as linoleum, rubber or PVC for hospitals is a staple material. Zealous cleaners often work hard on a high gloss to prove the environment is both clean and hygienic (Figure 2.60). However, the visually impaired often complain about the glare from these glossy surfaces and older people are nervous about slipping on the smooth surface. Non-shiny floor finishes are preferred; pale, matt floor finishes are available now that combine function and aesthetics (Figure 2.61). Plain, uniform patterns are less confusing for the visually impaired. Busy asymmetrical or geometric patterns on the floor are difficult to negotiate and have caused

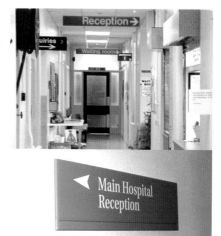

Figure 2.55 Visual noise and a cluttered environment can cause stress (top). Protect at least a few clear spaces (above) from the day-to-day mess of customised signage or abandoned equipment

Figure 2.56 Repair and refurbishments demand a stock of paints; a small number of conservative, generic colours are preferred

Figure 2.57 British Standard colours tend to reflect past interior colour trends however they are a useful standard for areas requiring regualr repainting schedules

Figure 2.58 A carpet achieves an immediate sense of quality and warmth underfoot, especially when used in an entrance

disorientation and even minor falls for some people who thought the design denoted a change of level such as a step (Figures 2.62 and 2.63) [2.26]

Designs incorporated in hard flooring to assist wayfinding are permanent so they require no upkeep beyond general maintenance. In one hospital, the use of darker boundary edges to the corridor, as part of a wayfinding strategy, has proved surprisingly successful in dealing with a major problem with wall damage from theatre trolleys. It produced a major saving in refurbishment as hospital porters found it easier to steer the trolley correctly with these darker boundary edges as guides [2.27] (Figure 2.64).

The current popularity of "wooden" vinyl, solid or laminate flooring has been filtering through to healthcare environments. The introduction of pale wood floors to waiting areas and wards has given some hospital environments a major uplift (Figure 2.65). Younger people prefer paler wooden floors and associate this type of flooring with modern environments. Successful technical developments in vinyl printing, which is both hygienic and aesthetically pleasing, have made a range of materials acceptable for clinical areas where wood or laminates could not have been used before.

Colour choice in flooring

All manufacturers of flooring have large ranges of colours so interior décor planning is easier than ever today. Paler flooring has been a major trend in flooring for a while in both soft and hard flooring. A pale colour will reflect more light, brightening up any space, but may tend to show the dirt more. A darker colour may mask dirt and not need to be cleaned so often, but it may show up lighter dust and debris normally hidden by lighter colours. The appearance of carpet, especially those with a smooth surface, will be affected by the reflected colour from interior walls or even a nearby building. It is a phenomenon that needs to be anticipated and is rarely easy to predict. Textured carpet on entry encourages people to wipe their shoes, which has the benefit of keeping other floor surfaces cleaner.

Any dark colour selected for this type of carpet will appear to be even darker than expected when laid because of the inclusion of textured shadow detail and the gradual build up of particles (see sub-section 'Optical colour mixing' in section 2.2). Always view the sample (especially if at some distance) in context, even more so if colour matching to details such as textiles or paint (Figure 2.66). Small patterns or designs will quickly merge at a distance, so any flooring with a small-detail design should be examined at a considerable distance in situ. This should avert any major colour coordination issues (see sub-section 'Optical colour mixing' in section 2.2). One rule of thumb is that warmer colours tend to dominate when optical colour mixing occurs. An amount of red of 25% for example such as a spot design in an overall blue carpet will appear to be more like 50%, producing a purple mix when viewed from a distance. Blue paint chosen to go with the blue background colour in the carpet may from a distance look very wrong with the purple mix.

Large areas of coloured, patterned carpet in a corridor can produce "tracks" or dominant lines and gaps in the design. This should not happen with high quality carpets if the repeat design has been carried out by experienced designers (Figure 2.67). But any problems in this area, unfortunately, are often not noticed until the final fitting has been carried out.

Figure 2.59 Coloured cotton mats which are absorbent can be machine-washed and tumble-dried

Figure 2.60 Glossy floors cause major glare problems for elderly and visually impaired people. Alternative surfaces should be used

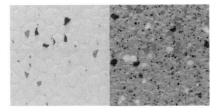

Figure 2.61 Pale matt flooring is desirable and can convey feelings of hygiene and comfort

Figure 2.62 Simple designs in flooring work best. Try not to use too dominant a geometric design which can cause disorientation for some people

Figure 2.63 Busy asymmetrical or geometric designs on the floor are difficult to negotiate and have caused disorientation for some people

Lighting of course has an impact on how coloured surfaces are rendered; the appearance of flooring is particularly susceptible to colour effects from different luminance types. This means that the correct selection of colour for flooring may need to be made very carefully under the exact light sources to be used, including daylight where applicable. The effects of different lighting on colour appearance of flooring can be checked with professional viewing cabinets that have different illuminants such as fluorescent or incandescent filament bulbs.

Figure 2.64 Wayfinding and colour-coding of corridor floors reduced wall damage from theatre trolleys in one hospital

Soft furnishings

These are materials used in bedding, linens, curtains, screens, cushions and upholstery. For patients, the materials immediately next to their skin, forming their bed surroundings, are the most important in creating a feeling of comfort and cleanliness. An important request by patients is for bedding and linen that makes them feel a little less institutionalised.

Textiles

Both the type of material used and the choice of colour can be very important and communicate a sense of quality and care. This will of course be specific to departments and the treatments being used in that department. In terms of textiles, for example, there is a preferred use of darker colours, such as blue for bed-linen in a dermatology unit (Figure 2.68).This obviates the stress for the patient of seeing ointment and skin-treatment emulsions staining the sheets, which can be embarrassing.

Figure 2.65 Paler "wooden" effect flooring creates modern bright environments used here in a treatment waiting area. These warmer floors are inviting and make the corridors appear less stark

Bed-linen

The colour, quality and appearance of hospital bed-linen with printed numbers or hospital names is often said to be fairly depressing for patients. Upgrading the sheets on beds in some healthcare buildings would improve patient morale considerably.

Patients are not the only ones affected by the poor textiles used; staff would also appreciate better quality sheets so that they could provide attractive and pleasing environments for their patients. Both staff and patients would like modern equivalents such as fitted sheets and duvets to ease the task of bed-making. It would also present a more modern feel to the ward, in keeping with current trends. Apart from white, the colours peach, green and blue are currently in use (depending on the type of ward) (Figure 2.69). Laundering maintenance is cited as one of the main reasons that more interesting colours are not widely used. Some managers say that mixed coloured textiles are uneconomical for this reason. This can leave some patients feeling very negative about their immediate environment.

Figure 2.66 View patterned flooring samples (above) in large sections in situ *to check visual result (top)*

However, certain textile laundering services have commented that they can cope with mixed coloured batches and only dark colours would create problems. Pastel colours related to zones of the hospital could be used to assist with a colour scheme [2.28]. Cream is a functional but clean colour which may not show much staining or soiling; yet it has been described as "homely" and recommended by some staff in NHS hospitals [2.24].

Bed garments have also been criticised for their low quality. Some staff have requested a need for better quality garments that are more acceptable for those patients who require them (Figure 2.70).

Figure 2.67 Vast runs of carpeting in corridors can often produce unexpected problems with design faults. The appearance of flooring is particularly susceptible to colour effects and changes from different luminance types including strong daylight

Blankets and top linen

Blankets and top linen are often seen by the patient and staff as important elements in creating a sense of well-being [2.24]. The blanket that appears to be in most general use is the cellular blanket; it may be either cotton or a mixed-fibre fabric (Figure 2.71). They withstand considerable laundering but deteriorate in appearance and need to be replaced before they become too worn out or dingy.

Many patients and staff would prefer thin, washable duvet-style covers for the wards. Staff cite "ease of bed-making" and the patients a "more homely feel" as their reasons for this. As wards are usually warm, a lighter version of a duvet could be used for patients and laundered when they leave the hospital bed. This would give the colour designer a chance to introduce some uplifting colours into the ward.

Colour can also be important on blankets or top linen to reflect softer colour in the immediate environment . Designers often underestimate the power of surface-reflected colour. In Figure 2.72, the difference between the two photographs, which were taken one minute apart, is the addition of a coloured duvet cover and the use of wooden blinds to reflect a softer coloured light. The introduction of colour to bed-linen would provide a much more uplifting ambience to the environment from reflected colours where clinically acceptable.

Upholstery

The choice of colours for materials used in upholstery should be based on practical and aesthetic criteria. Furniture adds to the overall impression of an environment and is usually a large and fairly permanent part of the building. Quality seating can help patients feel comfortable and at ease (Figure 2.73). The durability of the materials and textiles are very important as is the degree of wear and tear and location of the seating. A practical choice of colour linked to a technically tough man-made material which can at least be wipeable or waterproof is advisable.

The colour of furniture is a vital part of any scheme and contributes a considerable amount to the colour scheme. Wooden furniture comes in a range of colours from light beech to dark woods such as teak or rosewood, which can be included in any interior décor plans (Figure 2.74). Pale-coloured, fabric-covered seating, in yellow for example, has been reported as being damaged by the dye rubbing off from denim jeans.

Some patients requested additional cushions on seating for extra comfort, but it is seen as a luxury item that is primarily for visitors and seems to be more of a standard item in private hospitals (Figure 2.75) [2.25]. Fabrics would have to be easy to launder. Management of the tracking of textiles would apparently be quite difficult to organise across a large hospital complex.

Window treatments

For lighting and colour design, the most important element of a building in the daytime is the window. Daylight can be managed by the filtering of light by different types of blinds or sheer translucent fabrics (Figure 2.76).

Figure 2.68 Coloured sheets are often needed for clinical reasons; blue bed-linen is preferred within some dermatology units

Figure 2.69 The design and quality of linens offered for hospital beds is usually fairly limited. It has been said that this creates an unnecessary institutional, as opposed to domestic, feel to the wards

Figure 2.70 Hospital-issue bed garments are purely functional and need upgrading to match current user expectations

Figure 2.71 The quality of blankets and top linen are seen by patients and staff as important elements for a sense of well-being

At night, windows that are not covered in some way are essentially "black holes" and can be very depressing if the view has no illumination (Figure 2.16).

Vertical blinds can control light effectively, are not so prone to accumulation of dirt and can introduce some colour into the environment (Figure 2.77). The material and colour of either the blinds or the fabrics can create some surprising colour effects, which reflect off walls or beds nearby (Figure 2.72). Venetian blinds can reflect extra light into a room or onto a ceiling or wall. Wooden blinds can reflect a warmer coloured light into the room and might be useful for softening staff rooms or offices (Figure 2.78). In areas of the hospital which have poor external views or low levels of available daylight, the selection of window treatments can affect the atmosphere greatly (see section 3.1).

Curtains

Curtains are a staple material in hospitals and found in most parts of the building. They soften the environment visually and acoustically and in many cases form the divisions of interior spaces. In wards, curtains act as a wall or boundary between patients, providing a certain level of privacy. Care should be taken to ensure that patients, staff and visitors can appreciate the textiles. When lined, the curtains often have their lined side facing the patient (Figure 2.79). This has proven unpopular and consideration should be given to the use of fabrics which are reversible, woven or have some degree of translucency to allow light to filter through yet still retain some privacy (Figure 2.80). The designs of most woven fabrics have the definite advantage of looking attractive from both sides.

The healthcare environment is still to some extent dominated by floral textile designs (Figure 2.81). Whilst achieving a homely feel for some patients, the preferences of teenagers, children or men still need exploring judging from comments received. Excellent examples of textile designs which work well with the rest of a colour scheme in wards and dayrooms have been found from manufacturers. This approach helps to create a feeling of coordinated fabrics and décor that adds an air of modernity, quality and good design to the immediate environment seen to be missing from some hospital wards (Figure 2.82). Generally, it has been found that people appreciate and have come to expect a certain level of quality in design from environments beyond the bare minimum. Colour ordination can tackle this gap easily and have a marked effect on the ambience of an environment.

An interesting and imaginative example of local innovation in curtain design for a particular place is the curtain for a bedside found in a "home-from-home" birth unit (Figure 2.83). The sheer panel at the top of the curtain allows natural light to filter through to the patient whilst maintaining a certain level of privacy.

Figure 2.72 The power of surface reflected colour to change wall colour for example from coloured textiles (right) is often underestimated

Figure 2.73 A pleasant waiting area with carefully arranged comfortable seating can help reduce stress and give patients a little privacy

Figure 2.74 The appearance, material and colour of seating in an entrance makes a big impression on the people entering the building

Figure 2.75 Cushions are seen as a luxurious extra that confirms both comfort and care for the visitor or waiting patient

Figure 2.76 The use of different textiles can filter light and create a less harsh environment

Figure 2.77 Vertical blinds can introduce some colour and enhance the environment considerably especially if the views are urban and not scenic

Figure 2.78 Wooden blinds can reflect a warmer light into a cold room

Figure 2.79 Patients in bed are often looking at curtain lining which does little to brighten up their immediate environment

Figure 2.80 Translucent or woven curtains can provide visual interest from both sides without excluding light

Figure 2.81 Floral textiles have dominated the hospital environment for many years

Figure 2.82 New designs coordinating the textiles at windows with screens or curtains around the bed, as well as bed linen, are being developed to create environments of quality

Figure 2.83 Translucent panels at the top of these curtains provides some filtered light into a bed area within a maternity unit preserving privacy without excluding daylight

2.5 Examples of the use of colour in current hospital design

For many years, colour design specifications for hospitals followed a fairly rigid set of guidelines. The overuse of certain colours has led to an institutional feel at some of the older healthcare environments. However, some recommendations have been used wisely, especially where clinically important. In terms of ambience, colour has been used to create pleasing and welcoming environments with an atmosphere of cheerfulness and a feeling of calmness and well-being. Colour has created "welcoming", "homely" and "pleasurable" atmospheres, which were thought to ease the stress of patients. One way to do this is by the use of warmer colour tones and a more traditional approach to developing colour schemes (Figure 2.84).

A way to assist the selection and implementation of colour design in hospital environments is to look at good practice and current solutions. Many excellent examples exist on the NHS Design Portfolio web-site. The Portfolio [2.29] reviews both lighting and colour usage in healthcare environments. Colour has been used in four ways: creating ambience; identifying; architectural form enhancement; and decoration.

Colour is also associated with child-friendly atmospheres and was extensively used in children's hospitals to create colourful environments (Figure 2.85). Birmingham Children's Hospital describes its colour usage as "predominantly white walls and ceilings which are complemented by occasional bold, bright colours, supporting and reinforcing the atmosphere of cheerfulness encountered throughout the hospital" [2.29].

In terms of identity, colour was used to identify a variety of things including different levels of the hospital, different areas and zones within the hospital and routes for navigation and wayfinding.

Darenth Valley Hospital in Dartford, Kent (Figure 2.86), and the local secure unit, St Bernard's Hospital in Ealing/Southall, Middlesex, use a change of colour for zone/area identification.

Clevedon Hospital in Bristol (which employed user input in its design) and Newhaven Downs Developments in Brighton use colour for navigation/wayfinding.

Gloucestershire Royal NHS Trust in Gloucester uses a palette of 12 wall colours that stretch across the entire spectrum with varying strength or subtlety for the range of areas in a large acute city hospital for wayfinding.

Colour for architectural form enhancement has been used in the Bristol Royal Hospital for Children (Figure 2.87) where planes of colour were added to the external elevations to provide a distinctive image for the outside of the building. Sun-breakers on the south and south-western elevations were coloured on their underside giving vivid shades and vibrancy to the building's exterior. The colours of the sun-breakers were derived from the interior design where each level of the hospital has its own colour identity. The Bristol Royal Hospital for Children is one of the few designs to use user input, but it is not clear if colour issues were part of the user involvement.

Figure 2.84 Use of warm colour tones and "old fashioned" décor to give a pleasant "homely" ambience in a potentially stressful treatment waiting area

Figure 2.85 Colour in children's wards to provide a cheerful and uplifting environment with appeal for younger people is more widely used today

Figure 2.86 New buildings can use a change of colour for zone and area identification as seen on this entrance floor

PHOTO COURTESY OF NIGHTINGALES ARCHITECTS AND CHARLOTTE WOOD

Figure 2.87 Architectural use of colour at Bristol Royal Children's Hospital

The Radiotherapy Simulator Suite, Churchill Hospital, Oxford, extends its colour scheme into the external elevations, providing a distinctive image for the department within the hospital site.

In terms of decorative use of colour, examples of floor designs can be seen on the NHS Design Portfolio website (http://www.nhsdesignportfolio. nhsestates.gov.uk). Dawlish Community Hospital commissioned one local artist to advise on colour schemes used throughout the hospital. The same artist also created a decorative floor design featured within the main entrance.

The Tree House Children's Unit in Poplar Grove, Stockport, used a colour theme with particular emphasis on flooring (Figure 2.88), especially in the corridors and other communal spaces.

When using colour for decoration, Hove Polyclinic in Brighton was cautious, using only eight colours inside the polyclinic, thus creating an unfussy interior.

Generally colour schemes used by a wide range of healthcare establishments have been varied and specific to local or clinical needs. Some trends and preferences have been observed but mostly colour choices fall into fairly predictable patterns.

White, as has already been stated, is a firm favourite for obvious reasons. But, as mentioned previously, it is not good enough to be mentally stimulating for longer stay patients. Blues, greens and yellows have dominated the hospital environment for a long time because of tradition and also their calming influence (Figure 2.89) [2.7].

In the current round of audits, it has been seen that, generally, colour schemes have been themed around "cool", "warm" and "neutral". Cool colours would be soft blues and greens to complement what was once considered to be a typical complexion, flattering the appearance of those types of patients. With today's multicultural environment, this is less useful. However, these colours are cool and relaxing and very suitable for chronically ill patients. Blue is known to be a particularly favourite colour with people around the world and maybe the least visually demanding or disturbing colour that the interior designer has at their disposal (see sub-section 'Colour preference' in section 2.2).

Warmer colours, which include peaches, corals or pinks, were traditionally recommended for convalescence and maternity wards. In smaller areas, these colours helped create a more expansive environment. The ubiquitous colour magnolia [2.2], so popular over the past 30 years, belongs to this group. It has been popular for some very good reasons, including rationalising of paint purchasing and stock control; the colour is very easy on the eye, provides instant mellowness and can warm up any environment that is potentially grim. Thus, it has been successful in practice, if derided in theory. A wider range of colours that can do the same job are available to designers today.

Neutral colour schemes have become very popular in domestic interiors in recent years with an expansion in the use of beiges, softer greys and off-whites. Generally, this group is useful for making small interiors feel larger. However, for long-stay patients in hospital, these neutral, subtle colour schemes can be understimulating. But the use of greyed or shaded colours

Figure 2.88 A focus on colour for an outdoor flooring area provides a lively playground

Figure 2.89 The colours blue, green and yellow of all shades have dominated many institutional environments including healthcare. Blues and greens are calming, and yellow can provide brightness and optimism within an interior. However, an imaginative selection from these colour groups would dispel the institutional flavour of these schemes: softer grey-blue tones, pale-golds or light, dusky peacock-blues for example

can be effective for areas that need to be calming or subdued so that they recede, providing environments with peaceful visual surfaces.

Determining the success of the final result of a colour design scheme is essential. Asking the users as part of a post-occupancy evaluation strategy is the only way to gauge whether the desired result has been achieved. The colour-palette development and inclusion of existing materials is commonly found to be the biggest issue for many refurbishment projects.

Summary of Chapter 2

Colour design

Colour design for interiors covers all materials and surfaces.

Colour design cannot in itself heal, but it can aid the healing process and provide a sense of well-being.

Colour schemes should incorporate the finishes of appropriate existing features of the building.

Limit the colour palette: a lot of differing colours may lead to visual confusion and a feeling of unease.

Coordinate colours of all finishing materials (floors, walls, textiles and even noticeboards) for colour harmony.

Provide visual interest and distraction which becomes more essential for long-stay patients.

Do not overuse one particular colour. Blue and white tend to be preferred colours, but their overuse can lead to monotonous depressing environments.

Colour design and contrast for the visually impaired and elderly

Use colour design and contrast in the environment for the visually impaired and older people to comply with the requirements of the Disability Discrimination Act.

Help visually impaired and elderly patients by visually marking the changes in floor grade or slope, limiting usage of extreme patterns, and using pale, matt floor finishes.

Use contrasting colours for doors, their leading edges, door furniture and frames. Colour contrast need not be yellow and black.

Consider coloured handrails attached to a wall at waist height, colour contrast at dado-rail height and use colour-coding on floors.

Provide colour distinction between adjacent surfaces for enhanced visibility.

Improve the visibility of architraves, door frames, skirting and doors by colouring them differently. This will especially help visually impaired and elderly patients.

Colour design audit and colour scheme

Include existing material colours in the colour scheme to retain continuity in a refurbishment. If necessary, use spectrophotometer measurements.

Build the palette from the analysis of existing colours including building and finishing materials.

Observe all lighting conditions that may affect the appearance of the final colour of materials.

Pale colours should account for around 80% of the interior colour to reflect available light. Strong colours are useful for accents but the effects may be difficult to predict.

It may be useful to use a story or theme to create a colour scheme.

Colour is associated with child-friendly environments. The occasional use of bold bright colours can be effective.

Consider colour for architectural form enhancement in external elevations and shading devices.

Colour fundamentals

Colour controls light and reflected illuminance, so maximise this by using light colours wherever possible including exterior surfaces.

The change from day to night in terms of colour and lighting need to be given some thought when creating colour design and lighting schemes.

Colour matching should be done with care to avoid metamerism and problems with optical colour mixing.

Colour references and the principles of colour harmony are useful tools for the designer of a colour scheme.

Understanding the effects of colour, background and reflected coloured light on the appearance and appraisal of skin-tone health is important.

Wayfinding and colour-coding

The informed use of colour can help people find their way around a hospital. Signs can be presented in different colours for different parts of the hospital, although the colours should be chosen so that the signs are readable. Small areas of colour (for example, in skirtings and cornices) can highlight different areas. Finally, large areas (walls and floors) could be in different colours in different parts of the hospital.

Zoning with colours can be problematic and requires a minimum number to be really effective.

Consistency is vital in the design and implementation of all elements of wayfinding.

Large areas of strong colour should be used cautiously and colour blindness should always be taken into account when planning schemes.

Different tones or shades of the same colour should be avoided in coding, for example light blue and dark blue. People can become confused if the same words are used i.e blue. In maintenance and refurbishment, it is important for limited colours to be used, for the same reason that mistakes are easily made.

Identify why, and for whom, the colour-coding will be of use. Colour-coding for patients and visitors should be easy to comprehend with only a few colours. Colour-coding for the benefit of hospital staff can be slightly more complicated; staff should preferably be briefed on the issue.

Colour-coding should not dominate the visual environment. Try to limit the use of colour in a space (for example, on one wall of a corridor, instead of the whole corridor) or to specific features such as signage.

Contrast is vital for legibility for all in signage. Clear spaces around or near signage optimises recognition.

Colour and materials

Choosing colours from the British Standards palette might make replacement colours easier to specify during maintenance. Use hygienic, wipe-clean surfaces and finishes.

Pale, hard flooring and wood effects help maximise available internal light. Warm colour tones can provide a homely atmosphere and should be considered for bed-linens.

Window treatments have an enormous influence on the quality of light that penetrates the interior of a building.

3. Lighting and daylighting

Lighting is of critical importance in hospitals. An adequate level of lighting is essential if even basic tasks are to be carried out [3.1]. Lighting also has an important impact on running costs, with substantial savings being possible if energy-efficient, effectively controlled lamps and luminaires are installed, with maintenance being considered at the design stage.

But good lighting can and should be much more than this. Carefully designed lighting can transform the appearance of a space [3.2], making it attractive, welcoming and either restful or stimulating depending on the effect created. It can enhance the architectural appearance of the space and contribute to orientation and wayfinding.

Both daylight and electric light play a part here. In this chapter, daylight is considered first because it needs to be addressed at the initial building design stage.

3.1 Daylighting

Windows and daylight give a building a variety and interest that can rarely be achieved in any other way [3.3]. In surveys [3.4], people are overwhelmingly positive to the introduction of windows in buildings. There are three main benefits:

- Contact with the outside world, especially a view out.

- Light from the sky, which people tend to prefer to electric lighting in most situations.

- Sunlight, which is seen as therapeutic and invigorating.

Of course, windows have other non-visual benefits, such as fresh air. Where windows are provided, it is important that they are properly maintained: windows that are stuck cause unpleasant draughts; and where solar shading is damaged or missing they will be less well received.

View out

View out is particularly important for people in hospitals (staff and visitors as well as patients). It reduces feelings of isolation and claustrophobia [3.5]. It provides contact with the outside world and can add interest to the environment, particularly if things are happening outdoors. A view can also help people, particularly visitors, find their way around the hospital.

This contact with the outside may help patients recover more quickly. Wilson [3.6] found that twice as many patients in a windowless critical care ward developed post-operative delirium compared to a similar ward with windows. Keep [3.5] has found similar results. View out, rather than daylight, may be the most significant factor: Ulrich [3.7] found patients in a ward that had a view of trees recovered more quickly than those with a view of a brick wall.

The British Standard Code of Practice for daylighting [3.3] recommends that "a view out of doors should be provided regardless of its quality". However, most people prefer a view of a natural scene with trees, plants and grass and open space.

Windows should be large enough to provide a reasonable view. Window areas below 20% of the external wall are unlikely to give a satisfactory view. Above 30% area, however, people are largely satisfied [3.8, 3.9].

The most satisfying views include three layers: the immediate foreground, buildings or trees opposite, and some view of the sky [3.10]. This will vary with the eye level of the occupants. Figure 3.1 (reproduced from HTM 55 [3.11]) gives typical levels and an "ideal viewing zone" where there are occupants of each type (for example, in wards). In these situations, it is important that the window-sill is low enough to allow a view out to recumbent patients, and especially to children if they are likely to use the space. The ideal viewing zone may vary with external obstruction; where tall buildings are nearby, for example in courtyards, a higher window head is preferred to allow occupants some view of the sky and to let more daylight come in.

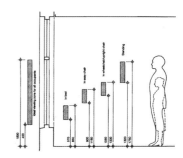

Figure 3.1 *Typical ranges of eye levels for occupants (to right of window) and the ideal viewing zone for all occupants (to left of window) [3.11]*

Where a space cannot be day-lit, special consideration should go to providing an attractively lit area with interesting internal views (for example, across an atrium) [3.3]. Small rooms with no view out or contact with the outside can be very claustrophobic [3.12].

Privacy is an important issue in many hospital interiors. Where the need for privacy may vary, for example in wards or consulting rooms, it is better to provide adjustable blinds or curtains rather than diffusing glazing. Diffusing glazing is more appropriate in toilets or bathrooms where there is always a need for privacy (Figure 3.2).

Light from the sky

Light from the sky is particularly important in hospitals. It gives excellent colour rendering [3.13], making many clinical tasks easier. It can also give significant energy savings by displacing the need for electric lighting [3.14]. The diurnal variation in daylight can help patients (particularly those who are in hospital for a long time) maintain their body clocks [3.15]. Daylight is also constantly changing as the sun moves round the sky and as clouds form and move about. This short-term variation gives variety and interest [3.16]. A lack of windows gives a constant environment, which is potentially boring and depressing [3.12].

To make the most of the daylight entering a building, the following strategies are needed:

Figure 3.2 *Glass blocks can provide natural lighting while maintaining privacy*

- Appropriate control of electric lighting is essential [3.14], so that lighting can be switched off or dimmed when daylight is sufficient (section 3.2 gives details). Controls should be zoned according to how much daylight is available.

- Choose shading devices and glazing so that daylight can still be admitted where possible (see below).

- Zone spaces so that activities which do not require daylight are located in the non-day-lit core, leaving other areas to be attractively day-lit.

- The distribution of light needs to be considered. Some hospitals have large areas of roof glazing concentrated in a few areas; this can cause localised overheating and make neighbouring areas look gloomy in comparison. But a smaller rooflight at the back of a predominantly side-lit space can help balance the lighting distribution [3.17] (Figure 3.3).

Figure 3.3 Use of a rooflight to the rear of a hospital ward provides additional lighting and improves the distribution of light

Current design guidance on daylight is contained in BS 8206 Part 2 [3.3] and the CIBSE Lighting Guide: 'Daylighting and window design' [3.10]. For day-lit spaces, they recommend the following:

a. There should be enough daylight in the space, quantified by the average daylight factor DF. A DF of at least 2% is needed for a space to appear day-lit, and at least 3% is recommended for most hospital spaces. However, areas with a DF much greater than 5% may be overglazed. Section 5.4 explains how to calculate DF. It depends on the area of glazing, on whether it is unobstructed and on the type of glazing. Tinted glazings often have much lower transmittances and give poorer daylight levels. A US study [3.18] has shown that when transmittance falls below 30–35%, people find the view out looks dull and gloomy. Highly coloured glazings may affect clinical judgments, especially where some areas are lit by electric light and others by light through the coloured glass. The daylight in a room also depends on how clean the windows are. Maintenance needs consideration, especially for roof lights and high level windows (safe access is a requirement of the Construction (Design and Management) Regulations).

b. The space should not be too deep. In a deep space, the interior will tend to look gloomy in comparison with the brightly lit perimeter [3.10]. In a typical side-lit hospital space, areas over six to seven metres from the perimeter (more if the window head is unusually high) will tend to look gloomy unless supplementary lighting is provided (Figure 3.4).

Figure 3.4 Areas which cannot receive direct light from the sky will tend to look gloomy. This underground car park entrance to an NHS hospital is an unfriendly start to a hospital visit

Each part of the working plane should receive direct sky light (Figure 3.5). Large obstructions outside will hinder this. This is a particular problem in courtyards [3.19]. The depth of the room that can be satisfactorily day-lit will vary with floor level. Near the ground, daylight will not penetrate far unless the window head is raised. Some improvement can be obtained if the courtyard surfaces are light in colour (Figure 3.6).

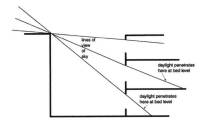

Figure 3.5 Daylight penetration in rooms off courtyards

Internal obstructions like equipment and bed curtains can also affect the distribution of light (Figure 2.83).

Glare from the sky can be reduced if the window wall is light in colour. Splayed reveals can also help [3.17] (Figure 3.7).

Sunlight

Opinions can be divided about sunlight. Longmore and Neeman [3.20] found that 91% of hospital patients questioned thought sunlight was a pleasure, while 62% of staff thought it was a nuisance. Patients like sunlight

Figure 3.6 Even if courtyards are internal and do not receive much light, they can give a view out and contact with the outside, particularly if planting is provided

because it gives light and warmth, and is seen as having a therapeutic effect; there is some evidence for this [3.21].

For many hospital areas, therefore, the appropriate strategy is to provide access to not only sunlight, but also adjustable shading [3.22] to control overheating and glare.

Access to sunlight will depend on window orientation and on overshadowing by obstructions. In general, spaces lit solely by windows facing within 45 degrees of due north will be perceived as poorly sunlit. Windows within 90 degrees of due north are also likely to give little sun if there are significant obstructions to the south [3.19].

For many low-dependency hospital spaces, curtains are the common shading option. Metallised fabrics are available which can reflect extra solar heat to the exterior and provide some extra insulation at night. For maximum daylight, it should be possible to pull the curtains fully back so they do not obstruct the glazing [3.17] (Figure 2.76).

Louvred blinds give better control of sunlight; often the blind can be adjusted to block sun but permit some view out. They are harder to keep clean, but provide good glare control, especially in non-clinical areas (Figure 2.78).

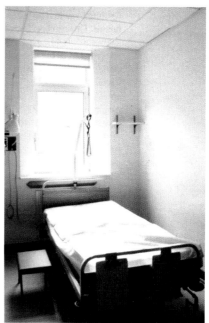

Figure 3.7 Splayed reveals surrounding windows can control sky glare by reducing the contrast between window and wall

The most hygienic option is to use mid-pane blinds in a sealed double-glazing unit. Mid-pane shading also rejects more solar gain than an equivalent interior blind [3.22].

In spaces with significant window area, extra shading may be required to prevent overheating in summer. Horizontal shading above the window, such as awnings, overhangs or canopies, can block high-angle summer sun while allowing winter sun and a view out [3.22]. High performance glazing is now available which can give reduced solar transmittance with a higher daylight transmittance.

Sunlight in outdoor spaces around the hospital is also valued, both for sitting out and to give pleasant views from inside. Asked if they would prefer a pleasant sun-lit view with no indoor sun rather than indoor sunshine with an unpleasant view, 50% of patients opted for the view [3.20]. Courtyards, particularly deep ones, are generally poorly sun-lit unless they are opened out to the south [3.13].

3.2 Electric lighting

Lighting design [3.23, 3.24] covers a range of issues (Figure 3.8):

- Task illumination: being able to see to move around safely and carry out tasks which may be simple or complex.

- Lighting appearance: providing a good-quality visual environment.

- Architectural integration with the design and the physical elements of the building, and particularly with daylight where it is available.

- Energy efficiency: including the specification of appropriate lighting controls as well as efficient lamps and luminaires.

- Lighting maintenance.

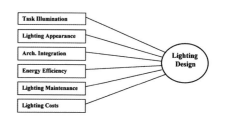

Figure 3.8 The components of lighting design

- Lighting costs, not just the capital cost of the installation but the running costs over its life.

The importance of each of the elements will vary, as will the solutions, depending on the particular application. For example, the requirements for a reception desk in an entrance area will be different from that of a nurse's station in a ward complex. It is essential for the designer to have a clear understanding of what goes on in each of the spaces for which the lighting is being designed. Chapter 4 gives more details.

The quality of the visual environment has a positive effect on the occupant's feeling of well-being and in the case of hospitals and healthcare buildings this can affect staff performance and patient recovery.

For example, harsh lighting has been identified as one of a series of stressors that can lead to episodes of delirium in a critical care unit [3.25]. In the neonatal ward, appropriate lighting can result in improved development [3.26], development of sleep patterns [3.27] and reduced retinal damage [3.28]. The elderly and partially sighted particularly benefit from good quality, low-glare lighting [3.29, 3.30].

Task illumination

In planning lighting for tasks (Figure 3.9), the first issue is to understand the nature of the tasks and to some extent the visual ability of the people concerned. For example, if the task is critical in terms of accuracy [3.1] and perhaps the detail is small, such as when applying stitches to an open wound, then lighting will need to be at a higher level, or illuminance, than for a less visually critical task such as moving equipment around the ward. Also if lighting is to enable patients to read and the patients are elderly with perhaps poor sight, then a higher level of illuminance will usually be necessary than if the patients are teenagers. For the actual amount of illuminance required, see the recommendations given by CIBSE [3.1, 3.31]. The following table indicates typical values. A range of values is shown to indicate that the particular situation needs to be considered, which will affect the actual value selected. Also to achieve the higher values, local task lights might be a good solution, rather than a high value of uniform illuminance.

Task description	Illuminance (lux)
Circulation areas (corridors night – day)	50–150
Reading (casual – critical)	200–500
Examination/treatment (minor – critical)	500–750

It must be stressed that recommended illuminance values apply only to the task area and not necessarily to the whole room unless the task is carried out anywhere in the room. There can be visual benefits to highlighting the task as it helps the person to focus on the work and improves visibility (Figure 3.9). Also there will be energy-saving benefits by not lighting the whole room to the same level unless absolutely necessary. But the designer must decide on what is required.

Colour representation (Figure 3.10) is another important issue in task lighting. In virtually all hospital situations, it is essential to be able to see surface and object colours accurately to avoid errors [3.32]. To enable this, the lamps used must be able to render colours accurately; and where

Figure 3.9 Different tasks require different illuminances from general ambient lighting (top) to focused task lighting at a workstation (above)

Figure 3.10 In wards, good colour rendering is vital to avoid errors in judgement of patient health

reflected light contributes to the task illumination, strong saturated colour surfaces must be avoided. The colour-rendering quality of a lamp is described by its CIE general colour-rendering index [3.1], usually described by the term Ra. The Ra scale has a maximum of 100 and for most hospital tasks a minimum value of 80 should be used, but where the task is particularly colour-critical, a minimum of 90 will be required. In theory, in areas where colour rendition is not critical, then lower values could be used, but experience has shown that where different coloured lamps are used in different situations, it is likely that they will be mixed up during maintenance.

Disability and discomfort glare [3.1] are potential problems and need to be avoided to ensure good performance. Disability glare is where there is a source of light, seen either directly or by reflection, which is so bright that it makes seeing the task impossible. Usually this can be avoided by screening all bare lamps from normal directions of view and ensuring that any bright reflected images are also outside the normal direction of view. Discomfort glare is similar although the offending source is at a lower brightness but still enough to cause annoyance and a reduced performance. Reflected glare can be a particular problem for computer or other screen-based users. However, modern screens usually have a diffusing surface that helps to minimise the problem. Problems of glare are not just the problem of electric lighting, but also daylight and particularly sunlight (see sub-section 'Sunlight' at the end of section 3.1).

Lighting appearance

The lighting of hospital tasks is important as is the lit appearance of the interior. There can be a conflict of requirements. On the one hand, there are high technology and critical tasks, some of which can have life or death implications. This suggests a crisp high-tech appearance, which will stimulate staff to a high level of performance. But on the other hand, the patients, particularly as they recover, may require a softer approach bordering on a domestic impression.

This same sort of conflict is shown in entrance and reception areas. The patient or visitor arrives wanting reassurance about the quality and care level of the hospital.

This can be demonstrated by the quality of the interior design, which includes the way the space is lit. But they also need to have clear direction to the reception desk, perhaps by making it the brightest part of the scene; here they are welcomed and directed to where they need to go next. If the lighting scheme is well designed, some of the apprehensions will be alleviated. Also if they have to wait in an unappealing space where the lighting has a functional appearance, they may become agitated and restless – a state unhelpful for a medical consultation or examination.

Some research has been done in this area [3.33] which shows that occupants like a room to have a measure of "visual lightness". But they also like measures of light and shade to provide "visual interest". The degree of these elements is determined by the use of the space. For example, you would not expect the same lightness and degree of light and shade for a sophisticated restaurant as a staff canteen. Research has also shown that lighting appearance is mainly determined by the brightness pattern of surfaces and objects in the most common area of view. This is the zone occupied by people's sight as they look horizontally. This includes walls and furniture but in large spaces, or wards where patients are lying down, this

Figure 3.11 In this day-lit entrance, high level suspended fluorescent fittings brighten the ceiling on dull days. Their cool colour complements that of daylight, contrasting with the cosier, warmer coloured lamps in the adjacent waiting area

Figure 3.12 Lighting complements colour design in this reception area. The downlighting highlights both the light wood flooring and the blue background to the desk. In the corridor area, fittings with a wider spread of light provide enough light to walls

Figure 3.13 Downlighting can be cosy and informal, but can lead to gloomy spaces with not enough light on walls and ceilings. Here extra wall lighting has been provided

will also include the ceiling [3.33]. Spaces with little light on the walls and ceiling will look gloomy.

To achieve a sense of lightness, it will be necessary to ensure that some walls receive some direct light – but not all walls, otherwise there will be no impression of light and shade and the space will appear bland and unappealing. As a guide, the average vertical illuminance within the normal horizontal sight-band needs to be about half of the task illuminance [3.33]. An important issue in designing for lighting appearance is to provide a pattern of light that relates to the architecture and application of the room in a meaningful way. The light pattern does not need to be obvious, but a natural element of the overall impression. One aspect of lightness is that it is not just the role of the lighting but also of the reflectance of the surface or object – it will be impossible to make a room that is decorated in a low reflectance colour appear light. This does not mean that you cannot use low reflectance colours, but they will need to be used sparingly if a light appearance is required.

A further element of lighting appearance is concerned with the colour appearance of the light. Electric lamps, particularly fluorescent lamps, come in a range of different colours, ranging from those that give a cool to those that give a warm appearance – this is described by a lamp's "correlated colour temperature" (CCT) [3.1] and is measured in degrees Kelvin (K).

On balance, since most areas of hospitals have daylight at some time, it is preferable to use a lamp colour that blends reasonably well with daylight but does not appear too cool at night. For this, a lamp with a CCT of 4000 K is recommended [3.1].

It is impossible to categorise in detail this element of lighting design because of the number of variables, which makes it important to commission an experienced lighting designer. However, Figures 3.11–3.14 indicate the general approach.

Architectural integration

This will include the following:

- Style of the lighting equipment with respect to the architecture (Figure 3.15).

- Meaningfulness of the light pattern with respect to the architecture.

- Physical integration of the lighting equipment with the building fabric.

- Integration of the electrical wiring, including controls.

- Integration of the electric lighting with daylighting.

Considering the style of the equipment is fairly obvious but this may be overlooked if the selection is left to the electrical contractor, who will often lean towards a functional solution. But equally, there can be problems if style is allowed to override performance; the equipment may look right, but will it perform as required? Both considerations are important, and a balance between the two is essential.

Equally, the light pattern produced by the luminaires must be meaningful [3.34] (Figure 3.16). For example, to direct a beam of light at a bare wall is meaningless, but to direct light at a picture, or some other object that

Figure 3.14 Lighting under the cupboards gives excellent glare-free task lighting in this drug-dispensing area. The standard ceiling lighting would not have been sufficient on its own, as the light to the task would have been shielded by the staff themselves

Figure 3.15 Selection and style of lighting needs to preserve and integrate with the character of the building

Figure 3.16 Scallop of light produced by a downlight. Here the placement of the picture complements the pattern of light, making it more meaningful

deserves attention, has purpose. Alternatively, if a line of downlighters were positioned close to a wall producing a scalloped pattern, then there would be meaning as long as the scallops were symmetrical and particularly if the wall had a textured surface. Sometimes it will be necessary for the architect to provide a reason for introducing a variation in illuminance, such as a change in floor or ceiling level.

It may also be necessary to introduce an architectural feature to incorporate concealed lighting such as a cornice or pelmet. The best solutions will be those devised jointly by the architect and lighting designer.

The physical integration of lighting equipment means considering things such as suspended ceilings and whether ceiling-recessed luminaires will conflict with other services like ductwork. The same applies to controls such as switches and dimmers. Early planning of where equipment should be sited and how it will be installed, as well as providing detailed instructions, will avoid problems later. Another consideration is whether walls are likely to be moved within the life of the building – if so then wire-less controls might be considered.

Integration of electric light with daylight is essential for optimum energy efficiency. This will mean assessing the daylighting performance and ensuring that electric lights can be controlled to complement daylight as and when required in a user-friendly way.

The overriding purpose of integration is to make lighting a part of the architecture and not a service fitted to the building after it is completed. Generally, the lighting installation should not be obvious but a part of the overall design.

Energy efficiency

Energy efficiency has a direct influence on running costs. But there is a second and more important aspect to energy efficiency and that is aiding the reduced use of electricity, which contributes to global warming and climate change. For these reasons, the Government has asked for a 15% reduction in hospital primary energy consumption by 2010, plus target energy uses of 35–55 GJ/100 m^3 in new facilities and 55–65 GJ/100 m^3 in existing ones. Lighting forms an important part of this. For example, a recent survey by a lighting manufacturer [3.35] estimated that if all the T12 fluorescent tubes in a large hospital were converted to T8, an annual energy saving of £27,000 could be realised; a substantial saving with just one measure. An estimate based on Building Research Establishment (BRE) data suggests that national savings of 80 GWh/yr, worth roughly £4 million annually, could be achieved by another simple measure, replacing tungsten lighting with compact fluorescent lamps in hospitals. A further 70 GWh/yr (£3.5 million) could be saved by the cost-effective deployment of suitable lighting controls.

Energy efficiency in lighting is measured in terms of the light provided and the energy it consumes. The light provided by a lamp is measured in lumens, the basic measurement unit of light. The energy it consumes is measured in watts, which includes not just the lamp wattage, but the energy consumed by any ancillary circuitry that is necessary to operate the lamp, for example a fluorescent lamp ballast. A lamp's energy-efficiency rating, or efficacy, is described in lumens per watt. But this only describes the lamp, whereas the efficiency of a light fitting, or luminaire, is also important. This is usually defined in terms of a luminaire's "light output ratio" (LOR) (Figure 3.17). This is the proportion of the lamp's light output that emerges from the luminaire in the directions required and is expressed as a decimal. Therefore, the efficiency rating of a luminaire is a combination of the lamp's efficacy and the luminaire's LOR. Lighting equipment efficiency is described in more detail in the 'Code for Lighting' [3.1].

Most hospital applications will use fluorescent lamps of either the linear or compact versions (CFL). Lamp colour performance has already been discussed, but for energy efficiency, linear fluorescent lamps of either 26 or 16 mm tube diameter, rather than the now outdated 38 mm, should be used.

Also the lamp ballast needs to be of the low energy consumption type with a CELMA rating of either A, B or C: this is marked on the casing. The CELMA rating supports the Energy Efficiency (Ballasts for Fluorescent Lighting) Regulations 2001 [3.36], which labels ballasts in terms of their energy consumption – A is the most efficient and C the least efficient.

Many modern lamp ballasts use electronic circuitry for improved energy efficiency, but they also often operate at high frequency which means that lamp flicker is very much reduced. This makes them much more comfortable for people who are sensitive to this effect [3.37]. Conventional low frequency fluorescent lighting may cause hum in some hearing aids, and this effect is reduced with high frequency lighting [3.38]. Also it can provide lamp-dimming facilities, which can be a useful facility in hospitals bearing in mind day-and-night operation. An important consideration with ancillary electronic equipment in hospitals is that it does not interfere with the operation of medical equipment [3.39]. This must be checked with equipment manufacturers before the commitment to specify.

Using energy-efficient lighting equipment is an obvious aim but it must be balanced by visual performance requirements. It also means only applying the lighting required for both the task and appearance, which does not mean flooding the whole areas of a hospital space with light that is unnecessary. The lighting installation needs to be designed to not only provide the lighting required, but also control it to the best effect [3.40]. Examples of this are switching lighting off when there is sufficient daylight or when rooms, or areas, are not occupied such as toilets and bathrooms. This will require the lighting circuits to be planned with this in mind. For example, zoning lighting circuits relative to the windows so that those nearest the window can be switched off while those furthest from the windows can be left on as necessary. Positioning and labelling of switches can help with this but in some cases automatic controls might be appropriate; however, for hospitals the designer must be sure that these will not interfere with the hospital's operation. The designer may like to seek expert advice on this complicated aspect of design; some guidance is given in Chapter 4. In addition, an Action Energy publication 'Energy efficiency in lighting', which gives an overview of energy-efficient lighting, provides useful additional information [3.41].

Lighting energy-efficiency measures are now included as part of the Building Regulations Part L and designers and users need to be aware of this and consult the relevant documents [3.42–3.44].

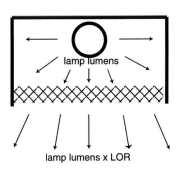

Figure 3.17 The light output ratio of a luminaire is the light flux that comes out of the luminaire divided by the lamp flux

Lighting maintenance

If a lighting installation is not properly maintained, it will deteriorate to the point where it ceases to provide the visual conditions required (Figure 3.18). Dirt build-up on the light-emitting and transmitting surfaces of a luminaire will mean that light is obstructed and it will cease to perform as intended; thus, energy and money will be wasted. Depreciation of the lamp can also occur, particularly with fluorescent lamps [3.1]. Although the lamp remains lit, its light output may deteriorate to below acceptable levels. If the installation is not maintained properly by ensuring that failed lamps are replaced promptly by the correct type and colour, or that damaged or defective luminaires are repaired or replaced, then the whole appearance will be one of neglect which could affect the performance of the department.

But lighting maintenance does not only apply to the electric lighting installation; it also applies to the cleanliness of the internal building surfaces, since in most lighting situations they will act as light reflectors. If they become dirty and lose their original reflectance value, some of the reflected light will be lost. Also, a poor level of decoration maintenance is likely to suggest a poor level of care and could have an effect on performance.

All lighting equipment will need to be cleaned regularly and at least once a year, but in some cases for purposes of hygiene this may need to be more frequent. To enable this to happen with the minimum of difficulty, it should be possible to reach the lighting equipment easily and safely with whatever equipment is necessary. But this must be considered at the design stage – too often luminaires are positioned in locations that are difficult to access and hence they are not maintained. If it is necessary to position a luminaire in a location that is difficult to reach, consider extra long-life lamps and totally enclosed luminaires.

The hospital will need to be advised about a maintenance programme, which should be supplied by the designer. They will need advice about lamp replacement and whether lamps should be replaced as they fail or whether there should be a group lamp replacement programme. Group replacement [3.1] can be a cost-effective approach where there are a large number of similar fittings. It can reduce labour costs and be carried out, along with cleaning, at a time to minimise potential disruption to hospital staff and patients.

It ensures that lamps that have depreciated to beyond their useful working life are replaced with new ones. In any case, the hospital will also need to be advised about stocking replacement lamps and any other replacement components and suppliers.

Lamps need to be disposed of with care, either to landfill sites or be recycled (not incinerated). Large quantities of fluorescent or other mercury lamps should be sent to specially licensed landfill sites or be recycled [3.45].

Windows and blinds will also need cleaning with a regularity to be determined by the cleanliness of the area. Proper safety procedures for this process will need to be ensured.

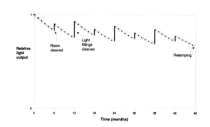

Figure 3.18 Light output variation over time as luminaires are cleaned and lamps replaced

Lighting costs

Like any other hospital building services, lighting has costs attached to it. They must be seen in context. The total capital cost of the electric lighting installation will be tiny compared with the cost of other building services and even smaller when compared with the total cost of the building. But unfortunately, lighting equipment is installed towards the end of a building programme when cost savings are often being sought. Pressure should be avoided to reduce the quality of the installation.

If the quality of the lighting installation is reduced, this could have detrimental effects on the operating costs. The life of a lighting installation will be ten years at least and often much longer. Therefore, if the installation uses more energy than it needs, because of less than ideal equipment, the running costs will be high. This will usually cancel out the apparent savings made through reduced equipment costs. The same thing applies to a costly maintenance programme, either through poor equipment that has a short life or through the need for complicated or difficult maintenance work. This means that the costs must be assessed through a life-cycle costing investigation [3.46]. It is important to adopt such an overall approach even when capital and operating costs are borne by two different organisations or budgets.

The remaining issue to be considered regarding lighting costs is that if good lighting is not provided then the staff will not be able to perform accurately and efficiently. Also if the quality of the internal environment is compromised through poor lighting, the recovery rate of patients could get worse. Both of these will be considerably more costly than the lighting – hence the necessity for a balanced approach where all the elements are considered.

Summary of Chapter 3

Daylighting

Choose window positions and dimensions to give a good view out wherever possible.

Size windows to provide enough light from the sky.

Choose appropriate shading devices so that patients and visitors can enjoy sunlight without excessive solar gain and glare.

Task lighting

Examine the particular task requirements.

Provide appropriate task illuminances for the task and the people carrying it out.

Use lamps with an appropriate colour-rendering property.

Avoid disability and discomfort glare from both electric light and daylight.

Lighting appearance

Aim for an appearance of "visual lightness".

Design for a pattern of light and shade to give "visual interest". Choose a meaningful pattern of light appropriate to the architecture and the application.

Consider the colour appearance of the electric light (typically a CCT = 4000 K).

Lighting integration

Consider the appearance of lighting equipment relative to the architectural style.

Consider the installation of lighting equipment relative to the form and fabric of the building.

Ensure electric lighting can complement daylight as required.

Energy efficiency

Choose energy-efficient lamps and luminaires.

Consider use of task lighting and an appropriate distribution of illuminance to reduce wasted light.

Reduce hours of lighting use by taking account of daylight and occupancy using suitable lighting controls.

Ensure compliance with Building Regulations with respect to energy efficiency.

Lighting maintenance

Set a regular schedule of cleaning lamps, luminaires and room surfaces for lighting performance and hygiene.

Ensure safe and easy accessibility of luminaires, windows and blinds.

Stock replacement equipment.

Develop a maintenance schedule including bulk relamping where appropriate.

Lighting costs

Use a balanced approach, combining capital and operating costs, over the expected life of the installation.

Capital costs cover lighting equipment, including controls, installation and commissioning.

Operating costs include energy and maintenance.

4. Hospital environment

4.1 Introduction

Different areas of the hospital will have a wide variety of colour and lighting requirements. This chapter divides hospital areas into three generic types: general areas, circulation areas and care areas.

General (public) areas consist of entrances, reception area, lobbies (and atria) and waiting areas, with their associated facilities. A hospital entrance is where the user first interacts with the building. It needs to be visible from outer approach paths and accessible to all. In lobbies, patients and visitors obtain the information they need about where to go and how to get there. A well-lit and relatively spacious lobby area, with a visible and accessible reception space, is important. Waiting facilities in these areas should provide a relaxing and calming ambience for patients and visitors who may be under stress. Facilities would typically include public telephones, toilets, retail outlets and restaurants or cafeterias (Figure 4.1).

Circulation areas include corridors, lifts, staircases and escalators. They are the intermediate spaces linking specific areas in a hospital to each other. It is important to have clarity of direction and enough visual interest in these areas to ease the stress of wayfinding (Figure 4.2).

Care areas (wards) include bedded areas, ward circulation areas, nurses' stations, day rooms, toilets and staff rooms. Wards are where patients are being looked after during their stay in a hospital. Wards should be reassuring; a feeling of excellence of medical care combined with physical and emotional comfort and an ambience that provides a feeling of warmth and relaxation are important to enhance the well-being of patients (Figure 4.3).

Specialist medical areas (treatment rooms, consulting rooms, operating theatres, laboratories, mortuaries, ophthalmological departments and radiography rooms) are not covered by this guide, nor is the specialist medical lighting used in wards. Lighting guidance for these areas is given in the CIBSE guide [4.1].

4.2 General (public) areas

Entrance areas

This is where the journeys of patients, visitors and staff in the hospital typically start and end; the first and last impression is created here. A high quality environment will instil confidence, giving an impression of quality of care (Figure 4.4) (see also sub-section 'Wayfinding' in section 2.3).

Figure 4.1 General, entrance and reception areas should be well-lit, with signage that is easy to read at a distance and designed to avoid confusion in wayfinding

Figure 4.2 Circulation areas and corridors should direct people and give some visual cues to ease the stress of wayfinding

Figure 4.3 Care areas and wards should reflect to some extent the comforts of the home with the reassurance of medical excellence

Current trends in new building for the healthcare sector make the entrance canopy an important statement, so both colour and lighting play a key role in signposting or landmarking this area with the appropriate NHS badging (Figure 4.5).

Modern building trends favour the use of glass and steel. These materials can cause problems because of glare and reflections; worse still, visually impaired people may not realise a glazed surface is there. Glazed surfaces need to be visible from outer-approach paths, usable openings or door handles being sufficiently identified by coloured or marked edges, or manifestations. This is especially important if automatic doors are installed to make the building accessible to all (Figure 4.6). Glare from steel can be less troublesome if coated or used with a brushed or pitted surface [2.20]

Figure 4.4 The entrance is an essential first stage of the wayfinding process. It should be 'badged' and highly visible

The inside of the entrance area needs to fulfil many functions. The main requirements are:

- As a re-orientation space for arriving and departing patients and visitors.

- A visible reception and information point.

- A minimum of essential directional information.

- A high standard of finish (Figure 4.7).

- Well-organised and uncluttered (Figure 4.8).

- A light and spacious atmosphere.

- Obvious cues for wayfinding.

Figure 4.5 For maximum visibility and minimal confusion, modern hospitals often make the entrance an important landmark with elements such as a canopy

The entrance can also play an important part in helping alleviate the fears and anxiety that children feel on entering hospitals (Figure 1.8).

"When you approach the main entrance it looks like you're coming to some really good science museum. It's got kites and different coloured flags on the canopy, and seagulls and a puffin. The entrance gives the impression that it's going to be a fun time. Well, maybe not fun, but it's certainly not going to be a horrible experience." [A 13-year-old patient about Derbyshire Children's Hospital]

Figure 4.6 Glass doors require adequate manifestations to alert people approaching glazed panels or doors from a reasonable distance

The locations of stairs, lifts or escalators also need to be clearly visible and recognisable from the main visitor and patient entrances in multi-level buildings (Figure 4.9).

Lighting

Illuminance levels in foyers should be carefully graduated. Near to the entrance, light levels need to be high so that the foyer looks welcoming from the outside and so that people can adapt on entering from the bright outdoors [4.2] (Figure 4.10). Different lighting levels can also be a guide to pinpoint main routes from the entrance to other areas or facilities.

Wall washing can make the foyer look bright and cheerful; avoid too much downlighting since the aim is to light vertical surfaces including signs and people's faces. Where the foyer may be continuously lit, use energy-efficient fluorescent or discharge sources. At night, lower illuminances are needed to make the foyer cheerful, so lighting controls should be provided with dimming, step-switching or programmable scene-setting (Figure 4.11). Emergency-exit lighting is also required.

Figure 4.7 The entrance area must fulfil many requirements. A high standard of design and finish inspires confidence and it should be accessible for all users

Colour design strategy

From daytime to night-time and through all seasons, the colour of the interior needs to be attractive and relaxing without being too stark (Figure 4.11). The selection of colours for this area is not easy, as all colours will have to be tested under the light sources installed or planned to be used in this sector of the building. Some beige or neutral tones can take on very unattractive green or orange hues under different types of lighting. What appears to be a very soft and neutral decor by day can turn into an unpleasant colour at night.

For identity, or to continue the exterior scheme into the interior, one large wall that has a statement colour can work really well. Yellow, although not favoured in many parts of the hospital building, could be used to provide a sunny, warm entrance area. The ideal surface on which to place a stronger accent colour is one that receives full daylight and also has provision for good night time illumination so it will not appear to be too dark. Bringing in external features of the entrance, such as paving or facing brickwork, into the main lobby area can be an interesting device to link the inside with the outside. Outdoor landscape planting can also be carried through to internal planted areas (Figure 4.12). This transition between exterior and interior is especially important in urban settings, where provision of natural features is limited. Glazing should allow one to see any planting outside easily, whether in tubs or window-boxes.

In terms of safety, obstacles or large areas of glazing will require adequate contrast and identification for users of the building, but especially for people with visual impairment (Figure 4.13; see also sub-section 'Colour design and contrast for the visually impaired and elderly' in section 2.1). Coloured manifestations on glazing will help to avoid accidents. Generally speaking, white sandblasted or etched manifestations on glass panels or doors are not of sufficient contrast to be useful for many of the potential groups for whom glazing can be dangerous [2.20]. The NHS corporate identity could be incorporated into functional manifestations on large glazed frontages throughout NHS sites.

Reception area

Once inside, visitors have to find their way about; this usually means a direct line of sight to the reception desk (Figure 4.14). The reception desk is the first point of contact in the hospital. It should contrast clearly with its surroundings. This means that the receptionist and the reception area need to be the brightest part of the visual field.

Since the visitor will be looking horizontally, the area needs a high level of vertical illuminance, particularly on the receptionist to provide a welcoming face. This is especially helpful to visitors who use lip-reading as a means of communication. For this purpose, lighting over the reception should be positioned between the visitor and the receptionist. Avoid heavy downlighting of the reception desk, as it can make the receptionist look sinister. But the receptionist also needs to read and write as well as use a computer, so lighting should be suitable for these tasks too.

Clear and uncluttered signage (see sub-section 'Signage' in section 2.3) can provide easy access to the rest of the hospital. Signage and lighting needs to work together to be effective. The front lighting of signage ensures maximum visibility. Visitors can then be independent, working out for themselves where to go. Colour design and lighting should maximise easy circulation for wheelchairs and trolleys.

Figure 4.8 The entrance should be well-organised and uncluttered from local customisation of signage

Figure 4.9 The location of stairs or escalators should be easy to see from the main entrance

Figure 4.10 The foyer of the hospital should look welcoming from the outside by day and night

PHOTO COURTESY OF NIGHTINGALES ARCHITECTS AND CHARLOTTE WOOD

Figure 4.11 At night the building's exterior should be illuminated to guide visitors from the distance of a car park or road junction

PHOTO COURTESY OF NIGHTINGALES ARCHITECTS AND CHARLOTTE WOOD

Figure 4.12 Plants or materials used externally can be effectively repeated and used internally, aiding the transition from exterior to interior; this can be particularly useful in urban settings

Facilities such as cafes or shops could also be included in this area, but should be clearly arranged so as not to interfere with the reception area. The reception area should be friendly and inviting for all the users of the building (Figure 4.15). Reception desks should be well-lit.

It is important to ensure that the reception area is accessible to people in wheelchairs and that counters or reception desks are suitable for patients in wheelchairs to be able to communicate with staff at computer terminals.

Colour design strategy

For visually impaired people, contrast and colour should be used to assist some immediate orientation. A combination of colour design and target spotlighting can help identify landmarks such as help desks, staff at an information desk and seating. Currently, designers are creating these areas to replicate the ambience of a hotel lobby (Figure 4.16). It should therefore be friendly and dignified. It would be sensible to start with a fairly neutral scheme which can accommodate the use of accent colours for zoning or wayfinding as well as elements such as lifts if they are part of the main circulation system of the building.

To avoid confusion and clutter, make sure notices or leaflet display stands are well located, are of good quality and are not scattered around haphazardly. The colour scheme in a reception area should be an extension of the entrance and bring the outside inside. Public seating may start here and for those that may require it urgently it should be accessible, easy to see and designed to provide a reasonable level of personal space (Figure 4.17).

Atria

An attractive atrium, of whatever scale, can make a big impression on visitors (Figure 4.18). Generally, the atrium will be well day-lit [4.3]. Patches of sunlight can add welcome liveliness, but too much sun produces excessive heat gains. Sometimes atria contain the reception or other working areas. A canopy enclosing these areas will control high daylight levels and make it easier to see any computer screens.

Lighting

Electric lighting in an atrium can be divided into three main groups:

i. Overall lighting of the whole atrium for use after dark or on dull days. This often uses high bay luminaires. Metal halide lamps give good colour. It is important that this lighting be mounted so that it is easily accessible for lamp replacement and cleaning. Induction lamps, which have an extremely long life, may be a useful alternative.

ii. Lighting for planting. Plants in an atrium or foyer [4.4] soften hard edges and give visual pleasure, "bringing the outside in". The feeling of a greenhouse effect with plenty of daylight requires careful design to be effective by night. Plants place large constraints on the lighting of an atrium (as well as affect its colour scheme) and the decision about which plants to include should be made early on in the design process. Littlefair and Aizlewood [4.3] and CIBSE's Lighting Guide LG7: 'Lighting for offices' [4.4] give recommended illuminances for various species of plants. Plants also absorb much of the light falling on them, lowering the average reflectance of atrium surfaces. They

Figure 4.13 Objects or areas of glazing which could be obstacles for the visually impaired or older people should contrast well with backgrounds

Figure 4.14 An attractive reception area should have an appropriate use of lighting and colour design and be in direct line of sight of visitors

Figure 4.15 A welcoming and well-signposted reception desk or area can make patients feel at ease on entering the building

Figure 4.16 Some hospitals try to achieve the atmosphere of a hotel reception area

need care in periodically cleaning the leaves and watering (Figure 4.18).

iii. Decorative lighting to highlight key architectural features within the atrium. This should be used sparingly to avoid high maintenance and energy costs. Highlighting of decorative elements after dark can be especially effective.

Appropriate lighting controls are particularly important in atria, because without proper control there can be very high daylight levels yet all the electric lighting may still be in use. Some form of daylight-linked lighting control involving either photoelectric switching or photoelectric dimming is often appropriate. These can be used in combination with occupancy sensing for situations where the atrium is less frequently used. Often, decorative "sparkle" lighting is left without automatic control, but it can look feeble and superfluous when sunlight floods an atrium. One solution is to leave it on a photoelectric circuit set to switch off under high, sunlight-dominated illuminances.

Even when daylight levels are very high, lighting may be left on along circulation routes because routes in the atrium are on the same circuit as those elsewhere, or for safety reasons. This should be unnecessary for properly designed photoelectric controls that default to "on" if the sensors fail.

Colour design strategy

In an atrium, colour will be subjected to extreme lighting conditions. All colours considered for a scheme should be extensively tested under all types of illuminance including full sunlight, low levels of light and near darkness. Any décor or artwork should be well supplied with the correct artificial lighting to maintain the same appearance and visual interest (Figure 4.19).

Colour design approaches can include:

- Well-illuminated sections of the atria with stronger colour in restricted places will give a lively feel to the space. Any stronger colours used should be wall-washed with light so that they do not darken at night and look grim.

- Plenty of warm, light colours will help reflect and bounce the light pouring into the centre. White can be harsh and cold; a slight tint can retain high reflectance levels while softening the light.

- Large white walls in some areas could be used as backdrops to dramatic, constantly changing, coloured projected-light washes; an economical way of introducing a gallery of colour and light to an exhibition space (Figure 4.20).

- Areas of coloured glass can have a similar impact, but they will look dark and featureless at night unless they are designed to be electrically lit from the outside (Figure 4.21).

- Background colours on walls or near reception desks can be developed from the materials used on the outside of the building. If they are seen through the glazing, colours echoing slate or red brick, for example, can create a successful transition from exterior to interior, or reflect some corporate or local influence.

Figure 4.17 Accessible seating which allows for private and personal space in the entrance area is important for both patients and visitors

Figure 4.18 Art, planting and good illumination in an atrium space can make a big impression on visitors

Figure 4.19 Mobiles in an atrium that are well-illuminated by day should be adequately supplied with lighting by night

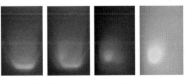

Figure 4.20 Wall-washing with coloured lighting can provide points of interest from a colour-changer light source

COURTESY OF ELGA NIEMANN

Waiting areas

Waiting in a hospital can be a difficult and stressful time, both for patients and for those accompanying them (Figure 4.17). Waiting can take place in a range of different spaces, from large areas in entrance lobbies to small special waiting areas for particular treatments (Figure 4.22). Furniture, colour and lighting can do much to alleviate stress and enhance those areas. Good design can provide a visually calming environment.

Comfortable seating with flexible configurations of small group arrangements could provide a friendly, welcoming atmosphere. Daylight and a view out, particularly of planting, make a waiting area much more pleasant and should be provided wherever possible. Figure 4.23 shows a newly refurbished waiting area in an NHS hospital that has been enhanced by the use of filtered daylight through stained glass.

Lighting

People often like to read while they are waiting; therefore, at least 200 Lux illuminance should be provided for this purpose, more if predominantly elderly people use the waiting area. Ceiling luminaires can be supplemented by wall-mounted lighting to add brightness to room surfaces and give a domestic-type feel to the space.

Consider typical viewing directions and the way the waiting space is used. Often, waiting patients are called for treatment by clinical staff who may emerge from the entrance to a care area or consulting room. When this happens, a good balance of glare-free lighting is important so that patients can easily see clinical staff and vice versa. Waiting areas also form part of the exit route in many hospitals, so the appearance of the area on exiting should be borne in mind. Emphasis of entrance and exit points, and signage, enhanced with additional lighting can help wayfinding.

Modern waiting areas often have television or computer screens to provide entertainment and information to patients. Lighting should be designed to avoid direct or reflected glare to those viewing the screen (Figure 4.24).

Telephones may also have illuminated text panels. Lighting should be positioned to avoid reflections in the display, but at the same time to provide glare-free illumination to the keypad. Colour and lighting in signage can help people to identify where telephones are.

Electric lighting may often be left on unnecessarily in waiting areas. Consider time-switching to ensure lighting is switched off outside occupied hours, coupled with photoelectric controls to make use of daylighting where it is available.

Colour design strategy

Creating a seating area which is not institutional in flavour is desirable to help people wait in a peaceful yet interesting atmosphere (Figure 4.25). Colour design and decor, along with drinks machines, photographs, magazines and television monitors can provide a welcome distraction. Attractive, well-maintained flooring could be light in tone and preferably warm in colour. For walls, fairly subdued hues that are slightly greyed are relaxing and pleasant and provide a foil for accent walls or features within the waiting area. These neutral colours can form a backdrop to stronger versions of the colours, used for example in furniture upholstery.

Figure 4.21 Coloured glass windows are stunning by day but need illuminating in some way by night

Figure 4.22 A waiting area in a treatment section where careful design and thought for the view out in an urban setting has been considered

Figure 4.23 Daylight through coloured glass gives this refurbished waiting area new life

PHOTO COURTESY OF EMILY ALLCHURCH

Figure 4.24 Wall lighting can brighten up a waiting area, but glare can be caused if it is placed too close to a TV monitor

A growing trend to use very bright PVC or linoleum flooring with inset designs has livened up many new environment refurbishments. In waiting areas, this device can be interesting and engaging (Figure 4.26). However, care should be taken with over-enthusiastic flooring designs as people may tire of too dominant a design and find these motifs unfashionable or even annoying after some time. Carpeting may be appropriate for these areas to give the seating area a more domestic feel, if maintenance considerations permit. However, near an entrance, polished hard flooring (vinyl, etc) is more suitable.

For adolescents and children the waiting area has to be an interesting place. For the very young, it will have to be entertaining as well as secure with adequate seating for parents (Figure 4.27).

Toilets

These facilities exist throughout the building, serving different groups from general public areas to patients' bathrooms attached to wards.

The colour scheme should always provide a good contrast between the sanitaryware and the walls to help all visitors see and use the facilities with confidence (Figure 4.28). A light reflectance difference of approximately 20% is required between walls or floors to assist visually impaired people using the facilities.

Compact fluorescent lamps are the ideal source for toilets because of their low wattage and size. They need to be positioned carefully to allow light down into cubicles. One or two luminaires should be placed near the mirrors to light people's faces adequately. The lighting and colour scheme should be very attractive to ensure that the colour appearance of people's faces is not depressing. Visually impaired users of hospital environments find using toilet facilities difficult if UV lighting is installed (UV lighting supposedly deters intravenous drug users who cannot find veins under it). Colours can be used for door handles or doors, which contrast with the surrounding wall colour to help people locate the toilets easily, without the need to find and touch surfaces (Figure 4.29).

Occupancy sensing is appropriate for occasionally used toilets. Sensors should be positioned to detect occupants at all times. A reasonable time delay (10–15 minutes) should be incorporated to prevent lights switching off while people are in cubicles. However, in most hospitals, the toilets will be in frequent use during the day. Over-frequent switching of the lighting can reduce lamp life. In these cases, a manual switch by the door may well be the best option.

Figure 4.25 A new colour scheme in this older but refurbished unit brightened up the waiting area. Colour schemes were developed locally by staff at the hospital

COURTESY OF NIGHTINGALE ASSOCIATES

Figure 4.26 Bright floor designs can revitalise an area such as this children's unit

Figure 4.27 Colour design schemes and good furniture are needed to produce an interesting children's waiting area

Figure 4.28 Contrasting walls from sanitary ware is helpful for the older or visually impaired to use wash-room facilities with confidence

Figure 4.29 Toilet doors and facilities should be easy to see and found quickly by all users of the hospital

4.3 Circulation

Hospitals can have a complex circulation system of corridors, stairs, escalators and lifts. The first requirement is to navigate successfully, not just to reach a particular point in the building, but also to find a way out of the building afterwards [2.17]. People need to visualise the layout of the building they are in (see sub-section 'Wayfinding' in section 2.3). In more complex hospitals, which may have gone through many changes and additions over the years, it may be hard to figure out the layout and understand how the spaces relate to each other [2.18].

Several techniques can help:

- Site maps, leaflets and signage might help to simplify the layout so people could relate to the architecture of the building. These should be consistent with the building layout, otherwise confusion can arise [2.18].

- Introducing clear and distinct landmarks to use as mental anchors along the routes [2.18] (Figure 4.30).

- Repeating information at intervals: users usually do not pay enough attention to the information available if they find it difficult to understand, and they tend to be forgetful.

- Open spaces within a building so that people can see what is above, below or ahead. External views out will also help orientation.

- A variety of architectural styles within a hospital complex also enables people to differentiate between the buildings to get their bearings [2.17].

- Simplifying the site by naming separate buildings, dividing large buildings into quadrants or wings, colour-coding different buildings, departments, entrances, floors or different parts of a building and using internal "street" names.

Developing different external views by exterior planting or create windows with solar shading or use sculptures.

Colour and lighting can both help here. Colour-coding (see section 2.3) is a powerful tool to differentiate between parts of a hospital. In circulation areas, colour-coding can be limited to signage or particular features such as skirtings, cornices and doors, or a wall and the floor can be a particular colour (Figure 4.31). Colour can be added to landmarks to help people remember them. Lighting should be designed to draw attention to signage – not to be a distraction from it.

In general, appropriate lighting controls are required in circulation areas. Day-lit corridors and stairwells can be fitted with photoelectric switching to reduce lighting use during the day; this will generally pay for itself in a short while. Little used circulation spaces can be fitted with presence detectors, although the positioning and choice of sensor needs care to ensure people never have to traverse an unlit space. It may be best to have one or two luminaires outside the control to ensure some light is always available.

Hospitals must have emergency escape lighting to switch on automatically in a power failure. This can best be achieved if the emergency lighting luminaires are an integral part of the normal lighting equipment rather than being separate, which can lead to unnecessary visual clutter. In some areas

Figure 4.30 Landmarks of any kind greatly assist visitors and patients with circulation and orientation. They also create points of interest which cross language barriers

Figure 4.31 Colour-coding could be integrated into a colour-contrast strategy used within flooring design such as this to aid visually-impaired users of the environment

of a hospital, it will be necessary, in the event of a power failure, to provide standby lighting to enable procedures to be continued or shut down safely. The level and duration of standby lighting depends on the circumstances. For detailed information on emergency lighting, see CIBSE's 'Code for interior lighting' [4.5] or BS 5266 [4.6].

Corridors

Corridors form the main network of circulation areas. For users, clarity of direction, visual interest, variety, landmarks and ease of wayfinding are the key issues for the successful design of corridors.

Long, straight corridors provide long vistas. If patterned finishing materials are used, for example patterned flooring, visual disorientation might be a problem when weaves or patterns do not perfectly match at junction points. Long corridors usually need some form of treatment, often colour based to increase visual interest, to decrease the monotonous feel to them.

Curved corridors are popular features of new hospitals. In a curved corridor, the view changes as you move along, which in itself provides some visual interest. But a curved corridor can make it more difficult to find where you want to go if a view out is not provided. Landmarks and colour-coding can help here. Refurbishments can improve long corridors if tackled with careful colour-design schemes (Figure 4.32).

En-route activities could be introduced with a "street" concept. Such a hospital street could be the focus of social interaction and gathering information with its galleries and arcades.

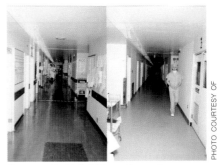

PHOTO COURTESY OF POOLE NHS TRUST

Figure 4.32 Refurbishments can improve long corridors if tackled with careful colour design schemes. Before (left) and after (right)

Corridors should be lit brightly but they do not require high levels of horizontal illuminance nor do they require high illuminance uniformity. There is currently a trend to use downlighting, either ordinary office luminaires or small, circular downlighters for corridors. But some downlighting luminaires can produce a gloomy sensation, and also downlighters do not light faces well. Downlighters can be glaring and disturbing to recumbent patients on trolleys.

Both problems can be alleviated by the use of wall-mounted uplighters to lighten the vertical surfaces of the circulation space. These can be arranged to fit in with the doors and other entrances onto the corridor.

An old-fashioned but effective solution may be to use ceiling-mounted prismatic or diffusing luminaires. Linear luminaires running across the corridor make it appear wider [4.2], but are less suitable for corridors with a lot of trolley traffic, and there can be bright reflected images from light fittings in the polished floor. An alternative arrangement is to use offset luminaires which predominantly light the corridor walls. These can give a light, airy feel to the corridor. The best arrangement for these will depend on the way entrances to the circulation space are laid out.

Windows are an important addition; they not only provide light but a view out, aiding orientation. They should be positioned at the side of a corridor and not the end; otherwise, people will appear in silhouette (Figure 4.33).

People need guiding where one corridor meets another at a T-junction. The arrangement will be very clear if the wall across the junction is brighter than the walls of the entry corridor; it will also indicate a change in direction. One

Figure 4.33 Windows which allow a view to the outside are helpful for orientation in corridors and provide a welcome distraction. Making these areas comfortable and safe for people to sit would be a benefit to the ambience of the building

hospital uses colour-coding that graduates from dark tones at the point where the corridor turns off to the ward to lighter shades at the final destination by the ward bed (Figure 2.13).

Care is needed where a corridor adjoins patient care areas that are used at night. Spill-light from luminaires should be avoided. The lighting level in the corridor may need to be reduced at night so that the visual transition from a darkened ward is less disturbing. This will also save energy and could be carried out using a timer switch.

Corridors are ideal for the implementation of any wayfinding device using colour. This can be on walls, dado rails and flooring to show intersections (Figure 4.34). A scheme of coloured doors can often liven up an area while using some form of colour-coding or zoning (see sub-section 'Zoning' in section 2.3). Colours can be used to lead the visitor to and from landmarks. However, too much colour is very distracting and can lead to people getting disoriented if the schemes are too vibrant.

Corridors could be designed with schemes that are not usable within clinical or waiting areas. They might be yellows or other warm tones which have more vitality than colours used for wards where restful tones might be used; this would provide some variety to the environment and also assist with orientation. However, the scheme should develop a strategy around one type of harmonic relationship (see sub-section 'Colour harmony' in section 2.2). It is best to avoid the use of a single colour in a corridor, especially a long one (Figure 4.35). This can seriously desensitise the eye, impair colour appraisal and produce unpleasant feelings. It is wise to include or introduce a complementary colour of some kind for visual relief.

The treatment of the corridor ceiling is crucial to the way one feels within the space. Ceilings are responsible for much of the ambience and are often overlooked. Lighting which washes up and reflects down can produce daylight effects. However, some methods to introduce visual interest (such as patterned ceilings) can provide disturbing, claustrophobic results (Figure 4.36).

Corridor floors which are highly polished can produce extensive reflected glare (Figure 2.7). This is not helpful for visually impaired people. If a patterned carpet is required, the design needs to be examined in situ with the correct luminaire to check for uneven patterning or unpleasant results of optical colour mixing (see sub-section 'Optical colour mixing' in section 2.2).

Lighting areas of wall with scalloped downlighter effects where specific strong colours have been used is a good way of providing clues to orientation and also providing interest along what can be quite boring traffic areas (Figure 4.37).

Stairs and escalators

Stairs can cause considerable anxiety to visually impaired users of buildings and those of limited mobility. The role of colour design in minimising these problems should be fully examined. All approaches to stairs and escalators should be marked well at the top and the bottom to warn people with visual and tactile clues that a change of surface is approaching. This can be part of an aesthetically pleasing colour scheme and does not need to be black to achieve enough contrast for people with low vision. Handrails are used

Figure 4.34 Corridors are useful places for implementing a wayfinding strategy. Floors are popular for this purpose. These changes in floor colour show where corridor intersections occur

Figure 4.35 A single strong colour in a corridor can desensitise, be disorienting and impair colour appraisal

Figure 4.36 A strong ceiling colour may add interest but can be overpowering

by people dependent on physical support while ascending or descending stairs. Many handrails are steel and should ideally have a satin finish to minimise shine and consequently glare. If coated and coloured, the material should provide high visibility of the rail and be sufficiently warm and tactile for lengthy physical contact.

Stairs should be lit well to provide a contrast between the treads and risers. Coloured, contrasting nosings or illuminated or luminous nosings (tread edges) can help safety (Figure 4.38). Bright luminaires or windows should not be located in the normal line of sight of people descending the staircase. These could cause glare and lead to an accident. It is important to check the visibility of stair colour and contrast on treads or step nosings by night. A contrasting side to the staircase can aid users to anticipate the rhythm of the steps by perceiving the zigzag profile. Generally, a light reflectance difference of 20% is enough to create a good colour contrast. Nosings are more commonly found in a stronger contrast such as black, yellow or white; but this may not be suitable for every harmonious colour scheme. Manufacturers should be able to supply a more innovative range of coloured contrast nosings for interior design projects.

Visually impaired people sometimes prefer ramps to stairs and a change of surface may be highlighted with colour or contrast (see sub-section 'Colour design and contrast for the visually impaired and elderly' in section 2.1).

Many people with low vision have stated that they would like to make use of lights often seen beneath the treads of escalators. The points of light give users confidence when using escalators. Although many advise against the use of steel because of glare, visually impaired people often use the glint or highlight from steel as guidance, although polished steel is much worse than a satin or sandblasted finish. Diagonal lines of the escalator handrails are particularly effective at attracting the attention of a visually impaired person. Having vibrant coloured sides to escalators can be a very good way to introduce interest and safety to the environment (Figure 4.39).

Lifts

Lift cars can be threatening and unnatural environments for the disabled, and particularly for those with mental health problems, because of their confined nature [4.7]. Lighting should make the lift seem bright and open; this can be done by illuminating the walls and ceiling. Control panels should be well-lit and care taken to design fully accessible signage, control buttons and instructions (Figure 4.40). Contrast on buttons and floor-level numerals as well as conventional tactile markings such as Braille are required. Avoid narrow downlighting as it will make the lift look confined and gloomy. The interior should be bright but not too bright as this will impede adaptation to lighting outside the lift. Contrast should be used for the external and internal lift buttons.

If lifts are part of the main circulation system of the hospital, the lift doors should stand out well from the surrounding walls. The doors should contrast significantly with the floor so that they are visible to all users of the building. If the lifts are central to a colour-coding or wayfinding scheme, that may determine the colours used but it should work from both inside and outside the lift. Achieving contrast for this area can liven up the immediate environment and need not involve the use of extreme colours. Colours used could be taken from the coding scheme (Figure 4.41).

Figure 4.37 Accent colour walls can be illuminated to provide visual interest in long corridors and main traffic areas

Figure 4.38 Colour contrast seen on approaching stairs and nosings help visually impaired people

Figure 4.39 Coloured escalator side-panels can be functional for accessibility, wayfinding and yet be part of a lively colour scheme

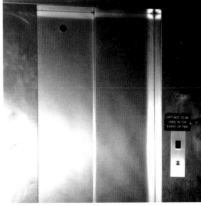
Figure 4.40 For older people and people with low vision, lift doors can be difficult to identify without any contrast and their controls are a challenge to use

4.4 Care areas

Wards

In wards, colour and lighting application can contribute to the efficiency of the staff and the welfare of the patient and the overall ambience for all users of the environment. The patient needs to feel cared for [4.8]. A delicate balance is required; an environment should make the patient feel that they are under modern and highly skilled medical care, yet be comfortable and relaxed enough to aid a speedy recovery or convalescence. The balance is not an easy objective to achieve.

Some key issues to be considered in a ward design, however, are:

- Visibility of patients from nurse stations and vice versa.

- Ensuring privacy or a sense of personal space for patients.

- Providing low noise levels.

- Satisfying patient control of their environments (for example, controlling incoming sunlight, bedside luminaires, the TV, phone etc) (Figure 4.42).

- Allocating enough space and comfort for visitors.

- Allowing natural light and views out.

- Design of an attractive and relaxing but not monotonous space.

An important point to note is that variations of types of colour schemes are required depending on the length of stay and type of patient, for example day ward, maternity, elderly or long-term care or paediatric (Figure 4.43). Provision of adequate visual stimulation for each type of patient and their length of stay will vary. In addition, a hospital ward usually deals with a particular medical condition, for example coronary care or maternity. Each ward will have its own special requirements which are not dealt with in detail here. The designer is advised to explore, in depth, requirements specific to the type of ward they are designing. However, a ward unit usually comprises a number of common spaces. These include circulation areas, patient bed bays, toilet facilities and staff working and relaxing areas. They each need particular treatment for their purpose but they also need to relate to one another in a coordinated way. A well-planned lighting and colour-design scheme can help achieve this.

Note: The CIBSE Lighting Guide 2: 'Hospitals and health care buildings' [4.1] provides specific information on illuminance levels and surface brightnesses. The designer is advised to consult this document for more detailed information.

Ward circulation areas

This will be the first point of contact with the ward for patients and visitors and it needs to convey a sense of optimism and clinical efficiency. During the day, it needs to present a bright and cheerful appearance so daylight should be included wherever possible. External walls are often limited, and the provision of windows onto the circulation areas is often not possible, particularly as other areas have a higher priority. However, with an open-plan-design approach, the awareness of daylight can be achieved, even if windows are some distance away. The view of a window, however small,

Figure 4.41 Lift areas on each floor can form part of the wayfinding colour-coding scheme in a hospital

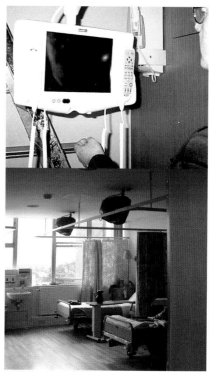

Figure 4.42 Patients not only require some control of their environment but need to feel connected to the outside world. Technology (top) or just a TV (above) helps patients remain in touch with life outside

Figure 4.43 Colour schemes should vary according to the length of stay and category of patient. This home-from-home maternity ward is vibrant to provide a lively atmosphere for a short-stay patient

will help to create a sense of lightness. This is particularly important for the staff, who often work in the centre of the ward unit, which is usually devoid of windows (Figure 4.44).

Lighting

Because circulation areas often have to rely on electric lighting, it is essential to use mainly high reflectance, matt finishes on walls and ceilings to form the basis of a light appearance space. The floor should also be a medium-to-high reflectance surface and have a matt finish to avoid reflected images of light fittings which could cause bright patches on the floor (Figure 4.45).

During the day, the floor should receive an average illuminance of 150 Lux to ensure safe movement, but at night this should be considerably reduced. This will help staff to adapt to the low levels of light in the bed-bays. It will also save energy. Electric lighting can be wall- or ceiling-mounted using fluorescent lamps, but they need to be carefully positioned, and of a limited brightness, to avoid discomfort to patients, particularly those being transported whilst lying on a trolley. The luminaires need to be selected and positioned so that at least some of the walls appear bright. Figure 4.46 shows one solution of wall lighting but notice how the patches of light relate to pictures and planting – this gives the lighting an added meaning and provides a natural extension to the architecture.

Colour design strategy

In traffic spaces, colour variety is desirable to create an interesting visual change of pace for visitors and staff. The use of bright colours for these areas will help compensate for any lack of natural light (Figure 4.47). Colours can also be used here to carry through wayfinding and navigation information, to create or identify landmarks, and confirm arrival at ward destination. This is particularly useful for users of the building who are unfamiliar with the site or the language used in signage.

In ward circulation areas, a lot of equipment and resources generally have to be accommodated in and around the nurses' workstation or just outside the bedded areas and service spaces. This section of the care area is usually full of visual noise with customised notices, signage, trolleys, directions for toilets and equipment (Figure 4.48). In the absence of adequately designed storage space, it may be best to create a few areas to take the bulk of this material, while preserving some visually tranquil areas.

Circulation areas are also perfect places to implement wayfinding and navigation schemes. This may be part of the specification and design of the floors. Carrying a wayfinding colour scheme through on one wall or providing coloured wall protection from theatre trolleys up to dado level is one way of breaking up an otherwise unrelieved space. Trolley damage to walls can substantially increase maintenance requirements. Placing boundary colours on the floor edges, largely used as a wayfinding device, has in one NHS trust hospital considerably reduced the damage to walls by providing visual cues to porters steering theatre trolleys (Figures 4.49 and 2.64).

Floors should be fairly light to reflect and avoid hiding dirt; visually impaired people can identify the outlines of people or feet more easily against a pale

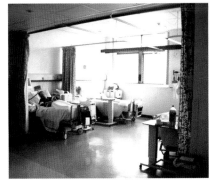
Figure 4.44 Daylight penetration through an open-plan-ward arrangement can be achieved through windows of any size which makes the most of potential lightness

Figure 4.45 Shiny polished floors create glare when illuminated with artificial lighting

Figure 4.46 Illuminated vertical surfaces and offset luminaires used to light a corridor space

PHOTO COURTESY OF TOMMY GOVEN, LIGHTING DESIGNER (FAGERHULT)

Figure 4.47 Colour schemes can brighten up the ward circulation area providing colour as a useful landmark for navigation

background. Some of the newer types of rubber flooring can be kept clean, yet retain a fairly dull surface to eliminate any harsh glare from over-polished surfaces. Light-wood-effect flooring can create an immediate sense of airiness and modernity to an environment (Figure 4.50).

Nurses' Workstation

This area is the hub of the ward unit; as it is a combination of reception desk for patients and visitors, office area, call centre and location for visiting medical staff, it needs to be visually prominent, particularly during the day (Figure 4.51). It also needs to accommodate a range of functions, ranging from communicating with people to a wide range of office tasks including the use of computers and storage of confidential information.

Lighting

There needs to be an adequate amount of light on the faces of the nursing staff manning the desk. This means using luminaires with some side illumination. Also projecting light onto the side or back wall can be helpful in making the area visually prominent. Office tasks can be illuminated using downlighters over the desk area – these can provide the required task illuminance of 300 Lux, prevent views of the lamps in the computer screens and avoid direct reflected images in horizontal tasks. An alternative could be to use local lighting attached to the desk. At night, the lighting levels need to be reduced. The range of tasks will be different. Some lights can be switched off. Task lighting could be reduced by using a local dimmer.

A number of lighting solutions have been suggested but it will be essential to ensure that all the lighting components combine to provide a coherent use and appearance. This includes the choice and positioning of luminaires and their control.

Colour design strategy

It is sometimes possible to coordinate the colour of the nurses' stations with the colour used in the corridor rather than the ward. A stronger hue than is used elsewhere in the care areas can highlight the station as well as provide a distinct and psychologically authoritative backdrop to the working area (Figure 4.52). The colour could be linked to wayfinding or zone-coding.

A general abandonment of the all-white environment for areas which require concentration and observation has become fairly standard. Experiments in the USA with colour in office environments found more mistakes and stress occurred in offices that were totally white without any relief from other colours [4.9].

The quality and design of the nurses' workstation can affect the efficiency and morale of both staff and patients. When refurbishing buildings, staff in some establishments have been involved in selecting furniture for their working environment (Figure 4.53). The overall design of this area is important to achieve maximum efficiency of the station for nursing staff and doctors.

The work surface should be such that the eye does not require much colour or brightness adaptation from tasks on the workstation to long distance viewing of the ward or patient areas. Generally speaking, a neutral

Figure 4.48 Clutter creates visual noise which is stressful for all. Protecting some free, uncluttered spaces can produce visually restful areas

Figure 4.49 Floor boundary colours created for wayfinding helped reduce wall damage from straying trolleys

Figure 4.50 Light flooring reflects all available light and creates a sense of space and modernity

Figure 4.51 The nurses' station is the hub of the ward and needs to be visually prominent, particularly during the day

grey of about 20–30% light reflectance is recommended, but the colour chosen should support the types of task that will involve colour identification. If cream-tinted paper were to be used as an office standard, a pale blue–grey would be an ideal background colour for a work surface. Extreme contrast in areas that are demanding on vision is not good and will cause problems with dark/light adaptation.

Ceilings can, however, be white to ensure optimum distribution of light. An area of softer, deeper tones on one wall will allow the eye to wander from close-focused tasks and have an opportunity for the eye to rest and look into the distance. A nursing station can at the same time be both a happy and a very stressful place. A colour scheme should be used which is soft and lively, for example greyed blues, greens or yellows (Figure 4.54).

Bed areas

These may be single or multi-bed units but the lighting and colour design approach will be similar.

Windows and daylight

Daylight and views out are crucial to aid patient recovery (see section 3.1). Patients have said that they do not care about the quality or context of the external view. Even watching people crossing a road is enough to reassure people that they are still connected to the outside world [4.10]. Not all views can be as striking as the window view shown in Figure 4.55.

Window-sills should not be too high in the wall for patients to be able to see out (Figure 4.56). Section 3.1 gives guidance here. Window-boxes can provide patients who are largely confined to bed with a pleasant view out despite a very urban setting (Figure 4.57).

The amount of daylight will depend on the layout of the ward and the number, size and position of windows. A minimum average daylight factor of 3% should be achieved wherever possible. The arrangement should provide most patients with an external view, even for those furthest from the window. This will mean controlling the use of bed curtains, which could obscure windows from some bed positions. (This also includes how the bed curtains are drawn when not in use.)

Older windows can be modernised and the light from windows in a new building softened by the use of blinds that tie in with colour schemes (Figures 4.58 and 2.77). The success of colour schemes for the ward or corridor leading up to the ward depends on how the room is lit and the transition from daytime to night-time (Figure 4.59).

Most windows will require blinds of some sort at some time during the year to screen direct sunlight or views of bright or overcast skies, which can be uncomfortable. Louvre blinds are often the most flexible. Light from windows near the bed area can be manipulated by curtains and blinds (Figures 4.60 and 2.76). Window blinds not only throw light into a room, but can provide an angled and tinted effect to the reflected light. Coloured venetian blinds can bounce tinted reflections around the spaces or walls nearby. This can add visual variety for patients who have to remain supine or where camouflage of external views is desirable.

Figure 4.52 A strong colour can be used successfully just behind the nurses' workstation, to signpost and make prominent key elements

Figure 4.53 Staff have the most relevant knowledge of their needs and should be involved in selecting furniture for their immediate environment

Figure 4.54 Nurse workstation colour scheme should be harmonious to give the eye a chance to rest

Figure 4.55 A view from a ward window – regardless of the type of scene (according to some research) – is a major factor towards a patient's feeling of well-being

Splayed reveals to the windows have already been mentioned (see section 3.1) These are particularly valuable in ward areas as they soften the brightness pattern between the inside and outside and can help reflect more light into internal environments. In some wards it may be possible to combine windows with roof-lights to produce an attractive pattern of light. Care should be taken so that these do not cause visual discomfort particularly to patients lying in bed. Figure 3.3 shows a successful solution.

Daylight can also help save energy. But energy saving will occur only if electric lighting is switched off when it is not needed. This means organising electric lighting on circuits that relate to the daylight distribution. Automatic controls can be used, although they may be seen as intrusive to the operation of the ward. Diligent staff can be a good alternative as long as they have been instructed on what to do and why.

Electric lighting

Electric lighting needs to be flexible in that it needs to have a restful appearance providing task lighting to allow patients to read or staff to carry out an examination or provide treatment. The distribution of drugs is particularly critical as labels need to be read accurately – this is normally done at the centre of the ward. At night the staff need to be able to check patients without disturbing them – a very low level of light is therefore necessary. Over the years, a number of ward-lighting solutions have been tried, some more successful than others (Figure 4.61), but the solution needs to be derived from the requirements of individual wards.

In modern wards, one solution that provides the range of requirements uses a wall-mounted fluorescent lamp luminaire that combines both indirect light from an uplighter and direct light from a downlighter. The luminaires are mounted over the bedhead at a height that clears the patient's head when sitting up in bed. The downlighter element needs to be dimmable so that a low level can be used at night and to be able to provide an illuminance of not less than 300 Lux on the patient for examination or treatment purposes. The uplighter component can provide a soft general illumination and be a supplement to the downlighter at night (Figure 4.62). It can also complement daylight when necessary. This enables uplighters furthest from the window to be switched separately from those near to the window – another energy-saving feature. Figure 4.63 shows an example of this type of lighting but there may be others that could provide the range of requirements. The brightness of these luminaires as seen from across the ward needs to be limited to avoid discomfort.

Special consideration must be made to how wards are lit at night when patients are asleep. This can usually be accommodated by installing small, ceiling-mounted luminaires equipped with a compact fluorescent lamp which directs most of its light downwards to light the central area to allow safe movement for nurses. Light sources need to be screened from the view of patients lying in bed. An alternative approach is to use low, wall-mounted luminaires, but care must be taken to avoid the light output being obstructed. The required average illuminance is 5–10 Lux at floor level.

The design of much of the lighting seen in hospitals has been distinctly functional. A chance to provide a feeling of domestic lighting at certain times of the day would be an enormous improvement to softening patients' immediate environment.

Figure 4.56 Windows should be low enough for patients who are confined to bed to be able to see out

Figure 4.57 A window-box can enhance the view from within the building enormously

Figure 4.58 Blinds can soften strong daylight and direct light further into the room

Figure 4.59 Designing the building lighting successfully for the transition from day to night is important for ambience

Figure 4.60 Different window treatments can filter and direct light and give patients a sense of privacy

Colour design strategy

Most building surfaces should be light-coloured to provide reflected light, which will help soften the light pattern. Ward ceilings are not always ideal when painted white. While white reflects the most light, a slight tint can reduce glare and promote comfortable vision. Special care needs to be taken with patients who are supine and can only see the ceiling. In fact, patients who are prone for long periods will appreciate a tinted ceiling related perhaps to wall colour with some subtle pattern or texture. The pattern must be subtle, otherwise it could cause hallucinations. Walls would probably be best treated with a colour which has 50–60% reflectance value and could be related to the ceiling tint. Walls away from the window may have go up to 70% light reflectance to compensate for less daylight. Window walls may contrast strongly with the bright window with the daylight streaming in (Figure 4.64). These walls should ideally be light and if the windows are very small the wall should be illuminated in some way to counteract the darkness of the surround. Floors should be light-coloured but a contrast difference in light reflectance value of at least 15–20% between walls and floors is desirable for people with low vision.

Another important function of colour is to flatter the appearance of the patient. Warm, cool or neutral colours can be used near the patient's bed and colour used should be chosen according to the type of ward. Short-stay wards need to be friendly, cheerful and upbeat and conducive to recovery. For long-stay wards, cool colours are recommended as they generally figure highly in people's preferences and are restful to the eye. These colours would prevent too great a contrast between mental alertness and physical incapacity.

Patients who are unable to move and may be surrounded by a high level of medical technology have a very restricted view; therefore, this area of the ward requires the utmost care to provide the right ambience with enough variety to maintain visual interest (Figure 4.65).

In general wards, a mixture of warm and cool colour effects may be used alternately to give a balance between feelings of excitation and depression. Another strategy is to use two or more colours and vary the combinations in adjacent rooms to provide visual stimulation.

Strong colours in wards can create a feeling of oppression and distraction for patients. However, it may be appropriate to use a limited area of a slightly stronger accent colour for coding wards. Pronounced patterns can be difficult to live with and are very disturbing. As a general rule, colours that do not have too much of a pastel shade and have a greyish tone result in a restful ambience, free of distraction. They are also practical in resisting soiling and abuse. Fairly subdued colours of this nature help to avoid emotional excitement but some variety is required to maintain a healthy visual balance. Newer buildings may contain much more standardised medical equipment which gives a greater uniformity of appearance. This requires care in integrating these machines with colour schemes (Figure 4.66). It may be possible to specify coating colours from the manufacturers of this type of equipment to coordinate with hospital and ward schemes (see sub-section 'Colour referencing' in section 2.2). This would add a feeling of quality to the environment.

Colours chosen for environments could negatively affect diagnosis of illnesses in certain areas in a hospital. Caution should be taken in using

Figure 4.61 In wards with high ceilings a successful approach has been the use of suspended luminaires to give a combination of uplighting and downlighting. The opaque sides to the luminaire limit glare to patients. Additional bedhead lighting is needed for patients to read by

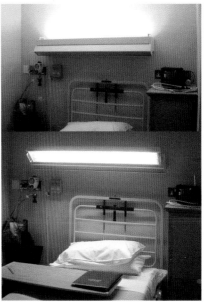

Figure 4.62 Traditional bedhead lighting is flexible for uplighting only (top) or for task lighting and medical examinations (above)

Figure 4.63 The bedhead luminaire can give combined uplighting and downlighting

blue in cardiac areas as this may hinder diagnosis of heart attacks [4.11]. Similarly, strong yellow colours in neonatal wards may hinder diagnosis of jaundice.

Similar caution should be taken whilst making colour choices in dermatology departments. Experienced hospital facilities managers report that hot (long wavelength, reds, yellows etc) colours negatively affect asthma sufferers and patients with dermatological disorders [4.11]. Aquatic, cool colours (short wavelengths, blues etc) seem to relieve itchiness in patients with dermatological disorders [4.11].

Green is also stated as being a good colour to use in floor-finishing materials, as it shows up body fluids, thus helping to prevent accidents due to slippery floors [4.11].

In paediatric wards, efforts to make the place feel appealing and colourful are appreciated by patients, families, staff and visitors. Often adult decisions on what children like can be wrong. A good mix of hues – both warm and cool – is a reasonable starting point for a scheme (Figure 4.67).

Use matt surfaces wherever possible to avoid reflections, which can be troublesome, particularly to patients lying in bed. The position of windows can cause a great deal of glare on a polished floor, which can cause problems for the elderly and visually impaired people. High level windows give good penetration of daylight to the rear of the ward, but their reflection in a polished floor can be disorientating (Figure 4.68).

Dayroom

Patients who are not confined to bed use the dayroom for reading, watching television or meeting their visitors. This area needs a domestic appearance, which can best be achieved by creating pools of light rather than a uniform illuminance over the whole room. There may be interesting visual effects in the form of artwork or special lighting (Figure 4.69). The limiting of information leaflets and general documents or notices to a specific area will help keep the place reasonably free of visual clutter; a dayroom should be an oasis.

These rooms should be day-lit, where possible, with an average daylight factor of at least 3%. They will also need blinds and curtains to help achieve a domestic impression.

Lighting

Electric lighting could be provided by wall-lights combined with standard lamps, although the latter can only apply if it is safe to do so. Safety obviously needs to be considered, hence the need to avoid long trailing leads by having floor-recessed socket-outlets. In cases where floor-standing luminaires are considered inappropriate, ceiling-mounted luminaires can be used. The illuminance level could range from 300 Lux in areas where people are reading to 100 Lux in areas in between. But it is important to aim for an attractive appearance so that patients are encouraged to use the room rather than staying in bed.

Fluorescent lamps can be used in most cases but will probably be of the compact variety (CFL). However, an appropriate colour performance should

Figure 4.64 Window walls can appear to be very dark with light streaming in from a window. Capturing light by the use of reflective surfaces nearby can alleviate some of this contrast. The dark–light adaptation problems for visually impaired people can be extreme in this situation. Extra care with colour and lighting for window walls can help alleviate this contrast

Figure 4.65 Bed areas can be bewildering places for patients and visitors with evidence of a high level of medical technology. Colour design can help soften these areas with pictures, textiles and coordinated schemes

PHOTO COURTESY OF POOLE NHS HOSPITAL

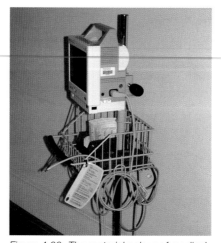

Figure 4.66 The material colour of medical equipment is not clinically important but it can contribute to the overall appearance of a ward. Manufacturers could look more closely at the colour and aesthetic appeal of such technical equipment. More provision for storage of equipment near the workstation would help staff keep the wards organised

be specified and that view of the lamps should be screened from normal directions of view. Lighting controls will need to allow a varied use of the light depending on the amount of daylight and the use of the space. Automatic controls could be used but they are probably not appropriate for this application as long as nursing staff are encouraged to switch them off when not required.

Colour design strategy

The dayroom should be very different from ward areas to provide enough variety to stimulate the mind (Figures 4.70 and 4.71). This can be achieved by alternating warm and cool colours between the ward and the dayroom. This should achieve enough difference to maintain interest and change or relief from the ambience of the ward. The hues used should be of high reflectance value but include harmonious combinations followed through with upholstery, textiles or carpets (Figure 2.30).

Bathroom and toilet facilities

These facilities are often given limited design attention because they are seen as a purely functional space, but they are much more than that. If a bathroom is neat and attractive, it will encourage its use and help patients to take an interest in themselves, which can be an aid to recovery.

Lighting

Lighting needs to be provided by a number of small sources rather than just one diffuser fitting mounted in the centre of the ceiling. Wall-mounted fittings, which are suitably enclosed to meet the required performance for a wet area, are a possible solution. In addition, lights beside the mirror encourage attention to personal appearance. Providing an attractive lighting scheme in toilets can also encourage better maintenance and cleaning (Figure 4.72).

It is common for lights to be left on in these rooms, so the installation of an occupancy switch could be an advantage to save energy. But ensure that it includes a reasonable time delay before it operates to allow users a safe exit and to avoid frequent switching when the facility is in high demand. Frequent switching of fluorescent lamps can cause a shortening of lamp life.

Colour design strategy

An environment that creates a flattering appearance of the patient is ideal. Good, reflective, light – but warm – colours are effective. The colour scheme should provide adequate colour and hue contrast and bring a varied colour palette to the area (Figure 4.73). If the overall scheme of the ward is cool in terms of colour and tone, a warmer colour may be a welcome change for the washroom. All sanitaryware should contrast with a background to achieve adequate "stand-out" for visually impaired people to be able to use the facilities with ease and confidence.

Staff rooms

These are the rooms where nurses and others can relax, catch up on support information like professional journals and make tea or a simple

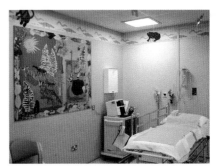
Figure 4.67 Children's wards should be vibrant and lively to encourage visual stimulation with discrete areas for changing displays

Figure 4.68 High-level windows can produce reflections which highlight polished floors

Figure 4.69 A comfortable dayroom with a photograph of a local area provides distraction and also reinforces a sense of community and place

Figure 4.70 Dayrooms should be clutter-free though interesting for patients to spend time out of the ward and experience a change in visual stimulation

LIGHTING AND COLOUR FOR HOSPITAL DESIGN

snack. In most departments they will be used throughout the 24-hour period by day- and night-shifts. Often staff will only be able to take minimal breaks in the staff room, so they should provide immediate visual relief and rest to enable them to gain energy for their work on the wards.

To reduce stress, the ideal staff room or lounge should be as different from other areas outside the room as possible. The staff room should be as homely as possible, but in line with current interior trends to bring the working environment up to the standard of other modern comparable workplace rest areas. It should provide quality time out of the wards and an environment that in even a few minutes can revive the tired employee. This is an important area where staff gain some valuable time in a hectic day or night, so the room needs to be attractive at night as well as in the day (Figure 4.74).

Improvements to staff areas appear to have a major effect on morale. Thought and care should be taken over the design of these areas where people are working for long hours and many years. The quality of these areas can indicate to the staff that the hospital cares for the workforce and rewarding them with an uplifting environment.

Windows will be appreciated even if they only look onto an enclosed courtyard, particularly if it has some vegetation. Curtains will be an advantage at night to shut out the "black-hole" effect. There should be space and adequate lighting for the display of plants or flowers that are always around the ward areas (Figure 4.75).

Lighting

Electric lighting needs to be varied and flexible to create light and shade. If a kitchen area is provided, install lighting under wall cabinets to light the food-preparation surface, cooker and sink. This will provide a good level of task illuminance for the tasks as well as aid a safe operation – it should also encourage cleanliness.

The sitting area needs to have appropriate task illuminances, for example 300 Lux where reading and study is taking place, but again it will be appreciated if this is not provided by a centre ceiling light. In some cases, the architecture will suggest solutions, but the use of direct and indirect lighting will form a good foundation.

The luminaires should be equipped with fluorescent lamps but screened from normal directions of view. Also ensure that all lamps have the same colour performance. The controls will be a combination of wall-mounted at the entrance and local switches as appropriate to allow a range of possibilities.

Colour design strategy

Local lighting can enhance subtle, warm-coloured walls and flooring. Providing varied lighting at different heights in the staff room creates an interesting and diverse environment akin to a domestic sitting or club room. Colours should be a set of related hues but of different strengths to accommodate different viewing positions of the staff pursuing different tasks. Ideally these colours should bring a colour or tone contrast from the ward or corridor. Whichever colours are used, a mellow ambient

Figure 4.71 A dayroom should feel ambient and be attractively lit; but the haphazard arrangement of furniture and wall displays with leaflets and notices can lead to a high level of visual noise through clutter which is anything but relaxing

Figure 4.72 Attractive wash-room facilities raise morale whether in the wards or general public areas

Figure 4.73 Toilet facilities can be part of colour schemes used throughout a ward. Using a contrast colour behind sanitaryware aids older and visually impaired people. A complementary colour from the harmony schemes would provide visual interest by a change from the ward colour schemes. This would be beneficial for long-stay patients

atmosphere can be created in any space by using the same colour scheme throughout the room (Figure 4.76). Upholstery should be coordinated with interior colours to create a feeling of a well-designed room. Textiles, curtains or blinds should all work in a scheme which softens the overall effect on all users of the environment.

Summary of Chapter 4

Reception

Use a foyer as a buffer zone between the bright outside and less well-lit interior.

Make the reception desk a clearly visible focal point.

Light the receptionist's face well; avoid heavy downlighting.

Waiting areas

Provide daylight where possible.

Use a combination of lighting to give an informal atmosphere and extra light on walls and ceiling.

Ensure lighting is glare-free for people looking in typical viewing directions (towards a central desk, or at TVs or illuminated displays).

Use light, warm colours for flooring and subtle greyed tones for walls as a backdrop to stronger colours for chair upholstery.

Circulation

Consider colour-coding and the use of landmarks to help navigation.

Use more than one colour in long corridors to provide variety.

Provide offset or indirect lighting to give a light airy feel to the corridor, avoiding glare for patients on trolleys.

At night, avoid spill-light to bedded areas. Consider dimming or step-switching to reduce corridor lighting at night.

Check the appearance and colour matching of patterned surfaces from a distance.

On stairways, ensure treads and risers are easy to see.

Provide windows, where possible, to help visitors find their way about the hospital. Consider photoelectric controls to save energy in day-lit circulation spaces.

Lift cars should be lit to appear more spacious and less threatening.

Emergency escape lighting is required.

Figure 4.74 Staff require a rest area that is as visually different from the ward and workstation as possible for maximum relief or concentration

Figure 4.75 Quality furniture in coordinated colours could create a less institutional oasis. Staff rooms should have different interior design treatment in terms of furnishings or colours to the wards

Figure 4.76 A thoughtful harmonious colour scheme with materials coordinating in some way will soften the overall effect of the environment on all users. Selecting a paint colour which matches or harmoniously contrasts with a permanent feature such as flooring or furniture can be a very successful strategy in economical refurbishments

Ward areas

Use appropriate colours for the type of ward.

Plan the layout of the ward and locations of windows and partitions so that some view of a window is available to staff working in the centre.

Dim or switch circulation area lighting to provide reduced illuminances at night, and avoid spill-light.

Wayfinding colours can be carried through into ward circulation areas.

Light the nurses' stations to suit office-type tasks but also to provide light on the faces of the nursing staff.

A stronger hue can be used to highlight nurses' stations.

Electric lighting should be switched or dimmed on circuits that relate to the daylight available in each area.

In bedded areas and dayrooms, the average daylight factor should be at least 3%.

Use blinds or curtains to control sunlight, but ensure they can be fully retracted when not in use.

Use matt, light-coloured building surfaces to provide extra reflected light.

In bedded areas, provide task lighting for patients reading as well as general lighting. A combined uplighter/downlighter approach can work well.

Colours should be chosen to flatter the patient's appearance. Avoid strong colours and loud patterns.

In day areas, compact fluorescent lights in a non-uniform pattern can provide attractive domestic-style lighting.

Consider alternating warm and cool colour schemes in wards and dayrooms to provide variety.

In toilets and bathrooms, provide enough contrast between walls and sanitaryware to help the visually impaired.

Consider a combination of light sources in toilets and bathrooms rather than a single fitting.

Provide windows and varied colour schemes in staff rooms to create a level of visual relief.

Consider a combination of direct and indirect lighting in staff rooms.

5. Resources

5.1 Troubleshooting

This section, compiled from comments provided by a wide variety of hospital personnel, deals with some of the most common problems that can occur, and gives hints on lighting measurement as well as some simple colour solutions.

Q. People are complaining that the lighting is too dim

A. There are three main possibilities here. It may that the lighting does not provide enough light to carry out the task. But it could be that there is enough light on the task but the space as a whole looks gloomy because other room surfaces are poorly lit. Alternatively, if the lamps are dimmer controlled they may be dimmed down too far.

Check first to see if the lamps are dimmed down. If they are fully on, then measure the illuminance on the task (see the end of this section for hints on measurement). If this is below the guidelines in section 3.2, then see below under 'Not enough light on task'. Otherwise look under 'Space too gloomy'.

Q. Not enough light on task

Check the lamps and luminaires are clean and do not need replacing. If they are, provide extra task lighting (see section 3.2). If a number of staff are complaining in the same area, consider installing more efficient, higher output background lighting.

Q. Space too gloomy

Measure the illuminances on the walls and ceiling to see if they are within the ranges recommended in Figure 5.1. If the ceiling illuminance is too low, consider installing extra uplighting to brighten it up. If the wall illuminance is too low, consider installing wall-washing. If both illuminances are satisfactory, consider redecoration in lighter colours, or fitting a lighter coloured carpet or pale hard flooring (Figure 5.1).

Q. Lighting too bright in daytime

Check that this is not a glare problem. If the overall lighting level appears too high (check by measuring) then consider installing dimming or step switching of the lighting, or at least flexible switching so occupants can switch off individual luminaires. It is worth noting that the illuminance is higher when the lighting is first installed or lamps replaced, and gradually reduces over time.

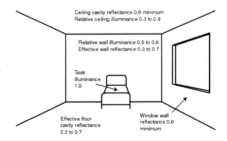

Figure 5.1 Recommended ratios of illuminances on walls and ceiling [5.1]

Q. Patients complain of night-time spill-light (for example from corridors)

Consider reducing the lighting in the corridor by selective switching or dimming, so long as this does not interfere with operational requirements. Alternatively consider installing some sort of baffle near to the luminaire, or between patient and luminaire (for example curtaining).

Q. Glare, or reflections in VDU screens or medical equipment

Try reorienting tasks and display screens to avoid the problem. Otherwise, consider replacing the luminaires to give better glare control (section 3.2). If the glare or reflections are caused by natural light provide appropriate shading devices.

Q. Lighting flickers

Inspect the lamp visually, particularly the ends of fluorescent tubes. If it is visibly flickering or flashing on or off, the tube or starter may need replacing. If there is little or no visible flicker, it could be that the occupant is especially sensitive to mains frequency fluctuations in the light. Replacing the control gear with a high frequency electronic ballast should solve the problem. Alternatively, move the occupant so they work mainly under daylight.

Q. Photoelectric controls don't work

This is usually due to an inappropriate setting of the potentiometer in the control. It may still be at its factory default level, or it could have been tampered with by the occupants. Under day-lit conditions adjust the potentiometer to give the right illuminance on the working plane. If it still doesn't work, check the photocell is not damaged, disconnected or covered up, and that photoelectric control is not disabled by the lighting management system.

Q. How can we create a pleasant environment in places with no windows, for example internal corridors?

With a carefully selected combination of a good colour-rendering light source and warm soft colour tone without any grey for example BS 10 B 15 Gardenia, a reasonable bright, warm environment can be created which will uplift any potentially dark area. A variety of positions of light sources such as wall-lights and task lighting will provide a bright, varied distribution of light which adds visual interest to an interior.

Q. What general advice do you have for selecting pale colours for large environments?

If possible you should always try to understand the source hue (for example, yellow, orange, yellow–green) for the tint of the colour you may want to use. Pale colours can produce surprising results in confined places. For example, a very pale yellow colour can be an orange tint, a yellow tint or a yellow–green tint. The source hue (orange or yellow etc) makes a very big difference when a complete room is painted in a pale colour. The internal walls reflect and intensify any pale tint. Understanding the source hue is therefore very important in predicting how colour behaves and intensifies in confined or large spaces. Most paint companies can provide the reference or notation for a particular colour you may want to use. Painting a sample colour inside a box will go some way to help in the judgement of a paint's final appearance in an enclosed space.

Q. How could the impact of contrast between old, existing scheme and a bright, new refurbishment could be minimised?

In many refurbishment schemes the retention of an old section is a fairly common situation. If a major part of the old scheme has to be retained for a length of time then one way of minimising the impact is to grow a new scheme from some of the reference points of the old. This might be a key colour from building materials or a feature such as moulding detail or a particular colour from fabrics or wallpaper. This will help integrate visually the existing environment with the new. The new scheme can be different but stands a chance of minimising the impact by relating the new scheme in some way with the old. An audit, to define the key elements of the old scheme that could be used as a reference point for the new approach, is a good way to plan a new scheme to lessen the impact of change.

Q. How do colour and contrast in environments help visually impaired or older people?

A level of contrast between areas or surfaces helps people navigate around interior spaces. Many people with low vision use the floor to scan and help orientate themselves so a good contrast between floor and a skirting or wall for example can be beneficial for guidance. Obstacles or hardware details such as door handles or wash basins should contrast with background colour (Figure 4.28). Further details are given in references 5.2 and 5.3 (see also section 2.1).

A majority of elderly or visually impaired people experience a lack of confidence in negotiating stairs or escalators. Contrast here to identify changes in surface is a critically and a legally vital colour contrast issue for DDA requirements.

Q. On colour design, how can maximum visual impact be achieved at little or minimum cost? Which features/elements give greatest individual impact?

With minimum outlay a carefully designed integrated feature can be created which provides visual impact and extra interest. Identify a particular area where a fresh focus of attention can be produced that has a function such as a wall in an entrance hall or a corridor, as part of wayfinding. This could be done by using a stronger saturated key colour developed from surrounding colour schemes, applied to a single wall which had wall-wash lighting illluminating the surface and could be repeated throughout a corridor scheme, integrated with a wayfinding strategy. Another way might be to add some decorative feature, such as textured surfaces or three-dimensional effects on particular sites. An illuminated, planted area or varied coloured display panels for notices would provide a very quick way to create some visual impact, tidy up unsightly areas and create visual interest.

Q. This room is "tired"; how can I make it look fresher by just using paint/colour without changing the whole room or colour scheme incurring considerable expense?

Many people do not realise how simply repainting the walls with the same colour can improve the environment immediately and have a beneficial effect on people's feelings of well-being. Identify the colours that were originally used on the walls by matching it with a colour in a current paint suppliers sample book. Most paint suppliers organise their paint samples by grading the colours from light to dark by additions of black and pale to bright by additions of colour. It will then be easy to choose a colour, one step brighter, lighter or darker than the current colour. Using a colour related to the old scheme but perhaps one step lighter or stronger in chroma can have a refreshing effect on the room without the need to change everything within the area such as carpets or furniture. Just creating a new colour on one wall may be enough.

Q. How can colour be used on doors to comply with the Disability Discrimination Act (DDA) and sit well with the colour scheme?

Choosing a door colour within a scheme which complies with the DDA is not difficult. A door colour may have enough contrast by being 15% different in light reflectance value than walls. All paint suppliers will provide data on the light reflectance value of colours. Alternatively architrave surrounding the door can be picked out in a darker colour and door furniture is now available in a wide range of colours and finishes. Open doors can cause problems for people with low vision who require contrast on the edges to avoid bumping into them (Figure 2.5).

Q. How can I use colour and lighting to make a room look bigger?

According to a Japanese study [5.4, 5.5], the brightness of room surfaces, particularly the walls, has a major influence on how spacious a room is thought to be. So in a small room it is important to have light coloured surfaces, especially walls. Light fittings should direct some of their light onto the walls. In a small room, downlighters with louvres to cut off light to the side can give dark walls feeling of claustrophobic space. Luminaires that emit some light to the side, or back washing (Figure 2.4) for example wrap around diffusers, will give brighter walls and a less oppressive environment. Alternatively, wall-washing fittings can be used as a supplement to task lighting [5.6].

Q. Could you give us some examples of good practice from NHS trust hospitals where colour design and lighting was used in refurbishments?

A. The pictures overleaf show the "before" and "after" of a recent refurbishment at Guys and St Thomas's Hospital, London.

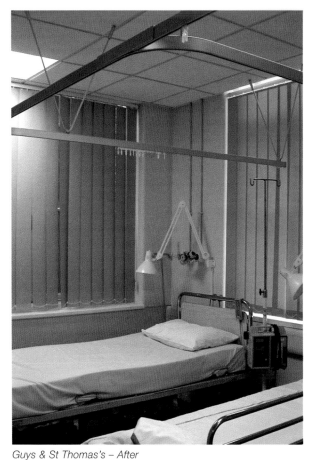

Guys & St Thomas's – Before

A fairly dark, old part of the Endoscopy Unit was targeted for refurbishment

Guys & St Thomas's – After

A bright but cool colour scheme using a violet-blue was chosen by the senior staff. With new vertical blinds, new ceiling lights and fresh paintwork the transformation of this once unappealing area has been appreciated by all users of the Unit and raised staff morale

Measuring lighting

It is useful to have a light meter (Figure 5.2) available to diagnose lighting problems.

Meters need not be expensive, but should have the following capabilities:

- The meter should be designed to measure illuminances in Lux. Exposure meters for cameras are not suitable.

- It should have a separate photocell on a long lead. Meters with an integral photocell are difficult to use.

- The photocell should be colour-corrected (to allow for the spectrum of different lamps) and cosine corrected (to allow for light coming from oblique angles).

- The meter should be properly calibrated by the manufacturers. It will need recalibrating every few years; check that the manufacturer offers this service.

Figure 5.2 A light meter with separate photocell

When taking the readings, the photocell should be properly horizontal (or vertical for measurements on a wall). Care should be taken not to obstruct the photocell with one's own body when taking readings. Measure both below and in between the luminaires.

5.2 Conclusions

In hospitals, a properly-designed visual environment, with the appropriate use of colour and lighting, will have important benefits. It can make the hospital experience more pleasant for a wide range of users from the elderly to the very young. Studies have shown improved patient recovery rates, linked to aspects such as window provision and appropriate lighting. This in turn boosts overall hospital productivity and staff retention in environments which are uplifting.

Hospitals are usually complex buildings, and they run more smoothly if people, both staff and visitors, can find their way about. Colour design is a powerful wayfinding tool if it is planned with care. Colour-coding, with a limited palette, can be used in signage and applied to building surfaces.

Lighting is about more than providing a particular task illuminance, although good task lighting is itself a valuable aid to productive healthcare. The appearance of spaces is also vitally important, and good lighting and colour design can make spaces look lively and welcoming instead of drab and institutional. Windows play a key role here as they provide daylight, sunlight and contact with the outside.

For both lighting and colour, a proper maintenance plan needs to be drawn up at the design stage, and carried out at regular intervals, if the quality of the visual environment is to remain high following installation or refurbishment.

Energy efficiency is an increasingly important issue. The use of efficient lamps, ballasts and luminaires, coupled with appropriate lighting controls, can be highly cost effective and help meet energy targets for the NHS.

In planning hospital environments (whether new or refurbished) cost projections need to take into account these running costs (energy use, ease of maintenance, staff productivity and patient recovery) as well as initial capital outlay. A relatively small investment in good colour and lighting design may reap major dividends over many years.

Colour design and lighting should be considered at a much earlier stage than currently appears to be the case. Their joint role in making environments inclusive for all users should be recognised by developers of healthcare premises.

5.3 Bibliography

References to Chapter 1

1.1 Chartered Institution of Building Services Engineers (CIBSE). Lighting Guide: Hospitals and Healthcare Buildings. London, CIBSE, 1989.

1.2 DiLouie, C. Quality Metrics. Architectural Lighting, Apr/May 1996, pp. 50–53.

1.3 Boyce, P.R. Human Factors in Lighting. London, Applied Science, 1981.

1.4   Lawson, B. and Phiri. M. Architectural Environment and its Effect on Patient Health Outcomes. University of Sheffield, 2002. See also http://www.hsj.co.uk/collections/be1.htm

1.5   Ulrich, R.S. 'View from the window may influence recovery from surgery'. Science, Vol. 224, 1984, pp. 420–421.

1.6   Shogun, M.G. and Schumann, L.L. 'The effect of environmental lighting on the oxygen saturation of pre-term infants in the NICU'. Neonatal Network. Vol. 12 No. 5, August 1993, pp. 7–13.

1.7   Ford, R. RIBA Conference. 'With design in mind'. 19 June 2002.

1.8   Birren, F. Color and Human Response. New York, Van Nostrand Reinhold. 1978, p. 23.

1.9   The Facilities Management Team, personal interview, Guy's and St Thomas's Hospital, London, 21 May 2002.

1.10   Loe, D.L. and Rowlands, E. 'The art and science of lighting: A strategy for lighting design'. Ltg Res & Technol. Vol. 28 No. 4, 1996, pp. 153–164.

1.11   Michel, L. Light: The Shape of Space. New York, Van Nostrand Reinhold. 1996.

1.12   Department for Transport, Local Government and the Regions, The Building Regulations 2000. Conservation of fuel and power. Approved Document L2. 2002 edition. London, The Stationery Office, 2001.

1.13   Fowler, E. US Research. Joint Commission Journal on Quality Improvement. July 1999.

1.14   Figueiro, M.G. Lighting the Way: A Key to Independence. New York, Lighting Research Center, Rensselaer Polytechnic Institute. 2001.

1.15   Kolanowski, A.M. 'The clinical importance of environmental lighting to the elderly'. Journal of Gerontological Nursing. Vol. 18 No. 1, January 1992, pp. 10–14.

1.16   Dalke, H., Cook, G., Camgöz, N., Bright, K. and Yohannes, I. Inclusive Transport Environments: Colour Design, Lighting & Visual Impairment. EPSRC/DfT Report. RNIB (in preparation), 2004.

1.17   Barker, P. and Fraser, J. Sign Design Guide: A Guide to Inclusive Signage. SDS & JMU Access Partnership. 2001.

1.18   Bright, K., Cook, G.K. and Harris, J. Colour Selection and Visual Impairment: a design guide for building refurbishment. (Project Rainbow). Research report, Reading, University of Reading. n.d. p. 9.

1.19   Royal National Institute for the Blind. Buildings and Internal Environments. London, RNIB, 1999.

1.20   Simpson, M. 'Lighting and the Disability Discrimination Act'. Proceedings of the ILE Lighting Conference, Sheffield, 2001. Rugby, Institution of Lighting Engineers, 2001.

1.21   Dalke, H. Colour design, lighting and safer custody in prisons. Home Office. (In preparation), 2004.

1.22   Baker, S. Environmentally friendly? London, Mind, 2000. Available from http://www.mind.org.uk/press- room/press_page.asp?ID=87

1.23   Disability Discrimination Act 1995. HMSO, 1995.

1.24   BS 8300: 2001. Design of buildings and their approaches to meet the needs of disabled people. Code of practice. British Standards Institution, 2001.

1.25   (The) Building Regulations 1991: approved document M: access and facilities for disabled people (1999 edition). Department of the Environment, Transport and the Regions. The Stationery Office, 1999.

1.26   Disabled Persons (Services, Consultation and Representation) Act 1986. HMSO, 1986.

1.27   Glass, P., Avery, G.B., Subramanian, K.N., Keys, M.P., Sostek, A.M. and Friendly, D.S. 'Effect of bright light in the hospital nursery on the incidence of retinopathy of prematurity'. N Engl J Med. Vol. 313 No. 7, 1985, pp. 401–404.

1.28   Mann, N.P., Haddow, R., Stokes, L., Goodley, S. and Rutter, N. 'Effect of night and day on preterm infants in a new born nursery: randomised trial'. Brit Medical J. Vol. 293 No. 6557, 1986, pp. 1265–1267.

1.29   Lindheim, R., Glaser, H.H. and Coffin, C. Changing hospital environments for children. Cambridge, MA., Harvard University Press, 1972.

1.30   NHS Estates, NHS Design Portfolio. http://www.nhsdesignportfolio.nhsestates.gov.uk

1.31   Revell, N. Teenage cancer crisis. Private communication.

1.32   King's Fund. Enhancing the healing environment. http://www.kingsfund.org.uk

1.33   Chartered Institution of Building Services Engineers (CIBSE). Code for interior lighting. London, CIBSE, 2002.

References to Chapter 2

2.1   Mazuch, R. 'Healing with design'. Hospital Development – The Journal for Healthcare Design & Development. August 2000, p. 11.

2.2   ICI Paint Library. Last updated 27 February 2003. http://distributors.duluxtrade.co.uk

2.3 Bright, K., Cook, G. and Harris, J. Selection and visual impairment: a design guide for building refurbishment. (Project Rainbow). Reading, the University of Reading, Departments of Construction Management and Engineering and Psychology. Np, Dulux Technical Group, 1997.

2.4 Colour Design Research Group, Kingston University, Knights Park, Kingston, Surrey.

2.5 Storring, M., Anderson, H.J. and Granum, E. 'Skin colour detection under changing lighting conditions'. Proceedings of the 7th Symposium on Intelligent Robotics Stems, Portugal, July 1999.

2.6 Mahnke, F.H. and Mahnke, R.H. Color and light in man-made environments. New York, Van Nostrand Reinhold, 1987, pp. 22–23.

2.7 Birren, F. Color and human response. New York, Van Nostrand Reinhold, 1978, pp. 100–109.

2.8 Camgöz, N. 'Effects of hue, saturation, and brightness on attention and preference'. Diss. Bilkent U. 2000. Ann Arbor, MI, 2001. http://wwwlib.umi.com/dissertations/fucit/3000379.

2.9 Wijk, H. et al. 'Color discrimination, colour naming and colour preferences in 80-year-olds'. Aging – Clinical and Experimental Research. Vol. 11 No. 3, 1999, pp. 176–185.

2.10 Saito, M. 'Blue and 7 phenomena among Japanese students'. Perceptual and Motor Skills. Vol. 89 No. 2, 1999, pp. 532–536.

2.11 Guilford, J.P. and Smith, P.C. 'A system of colour-preferences'. American Journal of Psychology. Vol. 72 No. 4, 1959, pp. 487–502.

2.12 Camgöz, N. and Yener, C. 'Effects of hue, saturation, and brightness on preference: a study on Goethe's color circle with RGB color space'. In Chung, R. and Rodrigues, A. (Eds), 9th Congress of the International Colour Association, Proceedings of SPIE. Vol. 4421. Bellingham, WA, SPIE, 2001, pp. 392–395.

2.13 Camgöz, N., Yener, C. and Güvenç, D. 'Effects of hue, saturation, and brightness on preference'. Color Research and Application. Vol. 27 No. 3, 2002, pp. 199–207.

2.14 Schuschke, C.H. 'Colour preference applying to patients and colour design in hospital'. Zentralbaltt for Hygiene and Umweltmedizin. Vol. 195, 1994, pp. 5–6.

2.15 MacDonald, L.W. 'Using colour effectively in computer graphics'. Computer Graphics and Applications. July/August 1999, p. 26.

2.16 Ford, R. RIBA Conference: 'With design in mind'. 19 June 2002.

2.17 Miller, C. and Lewis, D. Wayfinding: effective wayfinding and signing systems, guidance for healthcare facilities. NHS Estates, The Stationery Office, pp. 10, 14, 34–36, 71–99, 1999.

2.18 Passini, R. Wayfinding in Architecture. New York, Van Nostrand Reinhold, pp. 105–107, 194. 1984.

2.19   Tufte, E.R. Envisioning information. Cheshire, CT, Graphics Press,
        PP. 81–82, 89 1992.

2.20   Dalke, H., Cook, G., Camgöz, N., Bright, K. and Yohannes, I.
        Inclusive transport environment: colour design, lighting & visual
        impairment. EPSRC/DfT Report. RNIB (in preparation), 2004.

2.21   Minnaert, M.G.J. Light and color in the outdoors. New York,
        Springer-Verlag, 1993, p. 293.

2.22   Royal National Institute of the Blind. 24 February 2003.

2.23   Gill, J. Which button? Designing user interfaces for people with
        visual impairments. London, RNIB, 2000, p. 23.

2.24   Conversation, West Dorset Hospital, Dorchester.

2.25   Conversation – BUPA, Southend.

2.26   Centre for Accessible Environments CPD Course, February 2003.

2.27   Morgan, D. Director of Facilities Management, NHS Poole Hospital,
        Dorset, personal interview, 30 August 2002.

2.28   Conversation Laundry Services – Mr Phil Brierley (Service Manager)
        Sunlight Ltd. http://www.sunlight.co.uk
        Processing plant in Acre Lane, Brixton, London.

2.29   NHS Estates, NHS Design Portfolio.
        http://www.nhsdesignportfolio.nhsestates.gov.uk

References to Chapter 3

3.1   Chartered Institution of Building Services Engineers (CIBSE). Code
        for interior lighting. London, CIBSE, 2002.

3.2   Michel, L. Light: the shape of space. New York, Van Nostrand
        Reinhold, 1996.

3.3   British Standards Institution (BSI). BS 8206 Part 2: Lighting for
        buildings: Code of practice for daylighting. British Standard
        Institution, London, 1992.

3.4   Foregger, R. 'Windowless structures: annotated bibliography'. Bldg
        Environ. Vol. 32 No. 5, 1997, pp. 485–496.

3.5   Keep, P. 'Stimulus deprivation in windowless rooms'. Anaesthesia.
        Vol. 32, 1997, pp. 598–602.

3.6   Wilson, L.M. 'Intensive care delirium: the effect of outside deprivation
        in a windowless unit'. Archives of Internal Medicine. Vol. 130, 1972,
        pp. 225–226.

3.7   Ulrich, R.S. 'View from the window may influence recovery from
        surgery'. Science. Vol. 224, 1984, pp. 420–421.

3.8   Neeman, E. and Hopkinson, R.G. 'Critical minimum acceptable window size: a study of window design and provision of a view'. Ltg Res & Technol. Vol. 2 No. 1, 1972, pp. 17–27.

3.9   Keighley, E.C. 'Visual requirements and reduced fenestration in offices: a study of multiple apertures and window area'. Build Sci. Vol. 8, 1973, pp. 321–331.

3.10   Chartered Institution of Building Services Engineers (CIBSE). Daylighting and window design. London, CIBSE, 1999.

3.11   NHS Estates. Health Technical Memorandum 55: Windows. London, The Stationery Office, 1998.

3.12   Collins, B.L. 'Windows and people: a literature survey. Psychological reaction to environments with and without windows'. NBS Building Science Series. Vol. 70, Washington, National Bureau of Standards, 1975.

3.13   Henderson, S.T. Daylight and its spectrum. London, Adam Hilger, 1970.

3.14   Crisp, V.H.C., Littlefair, P.J., Cooper, I. and McKennan, G. Daylighting as a passive solar energy option: an assessment of its potential in non-domestic buildings. Garston, CRC, 1988.

3.15   Okudaira, N., Kripke, D.F. and Webster, J.B. 'Naturalistic studies of human light exposure'. American Journal of Physiology. Vol. 245, R613–R615, 1983.

3.16   Kendrick, J.D. 'Dynamic aspects of daylight'. Proceedings CIE Symposium on daylight, Berlin. Vienna, CIE, 1980.

3.17   Loe, D.L., Rowlands, E. and Mansfield, K.P. 'Daylighting of Nucleus hospital wards'. Proceedings CIBSE National Lighting Conf, Nottingham. London. Chartered Institution of Building Services Engineers(CIBSE), London, 1986.

3.18   Boyce, P., Eklund, N., Mangum, S., Saalfield, M.S. and Tong, L. 'Minimum acceptable transmittance of glazing'. Lighting Research & Technology. Vol. 27 No. 3, 1995, pp. 145–152.

3.19   Littlefair, P.J. Site layout planning for daylight and sunlight: a guide to good practice. BRE Report BR 209. Garston, CRC, 1991.

3.20   Longmore, J. and Neeman, E. 'The availability of sunshine and human requirements for sunlight in buildings'. J Archit Research. Vol. 3 No. 2, 1974, pp. 24–29.

3.21   Hobday, R. The healing sun. Forres, Scotland, Findhorn Press, 1999.

3.22   Littlefair P J. Solar shading of buildings. BRE Report BR 364. Garston, CRC, 1999.

3.23   DETR. 'Lighting for people, energy efficiency and architecture – an overview of lighting requirements and design'. Good Practice Guide. No. 272. Action Energy, Garston, 1999.

3.24   Loe, D.L. and Rowlands, E. 'The art and science of lighting: a
       strategy for lighting design'. Ltg Res & Technol. Vol. 28 No. 4, 1996,
       pp. 153–164.

3.25   Wilson, V.S. 'An identification of stressors related to patients'
       psychologic responses to the surgical intensive care unit'. Heart and
       Lung. Vol. 16 No. 3, 1987, pp. 267–273.

3.26   Graven, S.N. 'Clinical research data illuminating the relationship
       between the physical environment & patient medical outcomes'. J
       Healthc Des. 1997, pp. 415–19; discussion pp. 21–24.

3.27   Glass, P., Avery, G.B., Subramanian, K.N., Keys, M.P., Sostek,
       A.M.and Friendly, D.S. 'Effect of bright light in the hospital nursery
       on the incidence of retinopathy of prematurity'. N Engl J Med. Vol.
       313 No. 7, 1985, pp. 401–404.

3.28   Mann, N.P., Haddow, R., Stokes, L., Goodley, S. and Rutter, N.
       'Effect of night and day on preterm infants in a newborn nursery:
       randomised trial'. Brit Medical J. Vol. 293 No. 6557, 1986, pp.
       1265–1267.

3.29   Kolanowski, A.M. 'The clinical importance of environmental lighting
       to the elderly'. Journal of Gerontological Nursing. Vol. 18 No. 1,
       1992, pp. 10–14.

3.30   Figueiro, M.G. Lighting the way: a key to independence. Rensselaer
       NY, Lighting Research Center, Rensselaer Polytechnic Institute,
       2001.

3.31   Chartered Institution of Building Services Engineers (CIBSE). Lighting
       Guide: Hospitals and healthcare buildings. London, CIBSE, 1989.

3.32   Lovett, P.A., Halstead, M.B, Hill, A.R. et al. 'The effect on clinical
       judgements of new types of fluorescent lamp'. Lighting Research
       and Technology. Vol. 23 No. 1, 1991, pp. 35–80.

3.33   Loe, D.L., Mansfield, K.P. and Rowlands, E. 'Appearance of lit
       environment and its relevance in lighting design: experimental study'.
       Ltg Res & Technol. Vol. 26 No. 3, 1994, pp. 119–133.

3.34   Millet, M.S. Light revealing architecture. New York, Van Nostrand
       Reinhold,1994.

3.35   Molony, R. 'Hospital lighting: a national disgrace'. Lighting
       Equipment News. September 2001, p. 3.

3.36   The Energy Efficiency (Ballasts for Fluorescent Lighting) Regulations
       2001. Statutory Instrument No. 3316. London, HMSO, 2001.

3.37   Wilkins, A.J., Nimmo-Smith, I., Slater, A. and Bedocs, L.
       'Fluorescent lighting, headaches and eyestrain'. Lighting Research &
       Technology. Vol. 21 No. 1, 1989, pp. 11–18.

3.38   Simpson, M, 'Lighting and the Disability Discrimination Act'.
       Proceedings of the ILE Lighting Conference, Sheffield, 2001. Rugby,
       Institution of Lighting Engineers, 2001.

3.39   NHS Estates. Health Technical Memorandum 2014: Abatement of electrical interference, HMSO, 1993.

3.40   Department of the Environment. 'Electric lighting controls – a guide for designers, installers and users'. Good Practice Guide. No. 160. Garston, BREC-SU, 1997.

3.41   Action Energy. Energy efficiency in lighting – an overview. London, 2003.

3.42   Littlefair. P.J. 'Energy-efficient lighting: Part L of the Building Regulations explained'. BRE Report BR430. Garston, CRC, 2001.

3.43   Action Energy. 'Lighting requirements for Part L of the Building Regulations England and Wales'. Installers Lighting Guide No 4. London, Action Energy, 2002.

3.44   Action Energy. 'Lighting requirements for meeting the Technical Standards for compliance with the British standards (Scotland) Regulations 1990 – sixth Amendment'. Installers Lighting Guide No 5. London, Action Energy, 2002.

3.45   Sustainalite www.sustainalite.co.uk

3.46   Slater, A.I. and Davidson, P.J. Energy efficient lighting in buildings. Garston, BRECSU, 1992.

References to Chapter 4

4.1   Chartered Institution of Building Services Engineers (CIBSE). Lighting Guide: Hospitals and healthcare buildings. London, CIBSE, 1989.

4.2.   Illuminating Engineering Society of North America. Lighting Handbook. New York, IES, 1993.

4.3   Littlefair, P.J. and Aizlewood, M.E. 'Daylight in atrium buildings'. Building Research Establishment Information Paper IP3/98. Garston, CRC, 1998.

4.4   Chartered Institution of Building Services Engineers (CIBSE). Lighting Guide LG7. Lighting for offices. London, CIBSE, 1993. [NOT CITED IN TEXT]

4.5   Chartered Institution of Building Services Engineers (CIBSE). Code for interior lighting. London, CIBSE, 2002.

4.6   British Standards Institution (BSI). BS 5266 Parts 1–6: Emergency lighting. London, BSI, 1999.

4.7   Simpson, M. Lighting and the Disability Discrimination Act. Proceedings of the ILE Lighting Conference, Sheffield, 2001. Rugby, Institution of Lighting Engineers, 2001.

4.8   Mahnke, F.H and Mahnke, R.H. Colour and light in man-made environments. New York, Van Nostrand Reinhold. 1987.

4.9   Kwallack, N. 'Color psychology – it's not just black and white'. In Thompson, W. (Ed). Color and Design: 21st Century Technology and Creativity. Proceedings of the Inter-Society Color Council Conference. Williamsburg, USA, ISCC, 1998.

4.10   Ulrich, R.S. 'View from the window may influence recovery from surgery'. Science, Vol. 224, 1984, pp. 420–421.

4.11   The Facilities Management Team, personal interview, Guy's and St Thomas's Hospital, Borough, London, 21 May 2002.

References to Chapter 5

5.1   Chartered Institution of Building Services Engineers (CIBSE). Code for interior lighting. London, CIBSE, 2002.

5.2   Bright, K., Cook, G. and Harris, J. Colour contrast and perception; design guidance for internal built environments. University of Reading, 1997.

5.3   ICI. Colour and contrast – a design guide for the use of colour and contrast to improve built environments for visually impaired people. CD, ICI Paints, Billingham, 1997.

5.4   Inui, M. and Miyata, T. 'Spaciousness in interiors'. Lighting Research and Technology. Vol. 5, 1973, p. 103.

5.5   Inui, T. and Miyata, T. 'Spaciousness behaviour and the visual environment'. Journal of Light and Visual Environment. Vol. 1, 1977, p. 59.

5.6   Flynn, J.E. 'A study of subjective responses to low energy and non-uniform lighting systems'. Lighting Design and Application. Vol. 7 No. 2, 1977, p. 6.

Other useful publications

BRECSU. 'Energy efficient refurbishment of hospitals'. Good Practice Guide 206. London, Action Energy, 1997.

BRECSU. 'Electric lighting controls: a guide for designers, installers and users'. Good Practice Guide 160. London, Action Energy, 1999.

NHS Estates. Achieving energy efficiency in new hospitals. London, HMSO, 1994.

Barker, P., Barrick, J. and Wilson, R. Building Sight: A Handbook of building and interior design solutions to include the needs of visually impaired people. London, RNIB. 1995.
This book demonstrates how blind and partially sighted people may perceive the world around them, and shows how simple and low-cost solutions can make the environment more accessible.

Danger, E. The Colour Handbook, Gower, 1987.

Internet-based material

Building Regulations. The text of Approved Document L2 can be viewed on the ODPM website
http://www.safety.odpm.gov.uk/bregs/brads.htm.

CDRC – Colour Design Research Group
http://www.colourdesign.com.
Guidance on all aspects of colour design for the environment.

CADDET Energy efficiency in hospitals. CADDET Maxibrochure 05.
Available on http://caddet-ee.org/mb_pdf/mb_05.pdf

NHS Design Portfolio
http://www.nhsdesignportfolio.nhsestates.gov.uk gives a number of good examples of colour and daylighting design in hospitals.

King's Fund http://www.kingsfund.org.uk

Patient Experience
http://patientexperience.nhsestates.gov.uk includes information on the healing environment and wayfinding

Tiresias: an information resource for people working in the field of visual disabilities
http://www.tiresias.org

University of Reading
http://www.rdg.ac.uk/ie/ describes the work and publications of the Research Group for Inclusive Environments.

5.4 Glossary

Average daylight factor (DF) The average illuminance indoors divided by the unobstructed horizontal illuminance at the same time outdoors. The indoor illuminance is usually averaged over a reference plane covering the whole room.

DF is given by:

$$DF = \frac{W\,T\,\theta}{A\,(1 - R^2)}\ \%$$

where:

W is the glazing area.
T is the glass transmittance. Clear double or low emissivity glazing has T around 0.65.
θ is the angle (in degrees) of sky visible from the centre of the window measured in a vertical section through the window (Figure 5.3). With no obstruction, θ is 90° for a vertical window. Big obstructions outside can lower θ significantly.
A is the area of all room surfaces (ceiling, floor, walls and windows).
R is their average reflectance expressed as a fraction. In a light-coloured room, R is about 0.5.

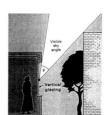

Figure 5.3 θ is the angle of sky visible from the centre of the window, in a vertical plane at right-angles to the window wall

Ballast A device to limit the current through a lamp (such as a fluorescent lamp).

Brightness The subjective response to the amount of light per unit area emitted or reflected in the direction of the viewer by a surface.

Chroma An index of saturation or strength of colour ranging from 0 for neutral grey or no colour to 10 or over for stronger colours as seen in the Munsell System or 0–100% in the NCS system.

CIE The Commission Internationale d'Eclairage (International Commission on Illumination), the international body responsible for lighting matters.

CIELab A three-dimensional geometric representation of colours in space (Figure 2.21). Equal distances in the space represent approximately equal differences in perceived colour.

Colour measurement The measurement of surface colour is possible with a spectrophotometer. This provides a CIELab reference which is universally understood. Widely used in industry as a quality control or matching process.

Colour references Commercially developed and established systems for organising colours in a range for easy access and colour communication.

Colour rendering A general expression for the appearance of surface colour when illuminated by light from a given source compared, consciously or unconsciously, with their appearance under light from some reference source. Good colour rendering implies similarity of appearance to being under daylight.

Colourways A set of colours used in a patterned textile. The colours can be replaced by a new set which re-colours the design in essentially the same way but with a new set of colours or colourway.

Contrast The difference in tonal appearance between two parts of the visual field seen simultaneously or successively. Boundary edges of two samples contrast when the samples have enough contrast between them to be seen as different samples. (See "Light reflectance value").

Correlated Colour Temperature (CCT) The temperature of a full radiator which emits radiation having the nearest colour to that of the light source being considered, for example the colour of a full radiator at 3500 K is the nearest match to that of a white tubular fluorescent lamp.

Font The style of the text or typeface. For example, Times New Roman (serif) or Arial (sans-serif).

Glare The discomfort or impairment of vision experienced when parts of the visual field are excessively bright in relation to their surroundings. Disability glare is glare produced directly or by reflection that impairs the vision of objects without necessarily causing discomfort. Discomfort glare is glare that causes discomfort without impairing the ability to see an object. Some visually impaired people experience physical pain from glare.

Harmony Structured relationships between colours. Opposite or adjacent hues or variations in tonal (brightness or value) scales of a single colour will all have a harmonic relationship between the colours

Hue The colour name in the sense of Red, Yellow, Green etc.

Illuminance The amount of light falling on a surface per unit area, measured in Lux.

Light reflectance value See "Reflectance".

Luminaire A light fitting.

Manifestations The graphic motifs, patterns or devices used on glazing to alert people to the fact that the surface ahead is transparent or glass.

Metamerism The phenomenon occurring when coloured objects which match under one illuminant do not match under another due to fundamental component differences such as pigment source.

Munsell System A system of surface colour classification using uniform colour scales of hue, colour and chroma. A typical Munsell designation of a colour is 7.5 BG6/2, where 7.5BG (blue/green) is the hue reference, 6 is the value or brightness and 2 is the chroma or saturation reference number.

Optical colour mixing This differs from mixing of solid pigments. Small dots of different colours mix optically in a very unpredictable way when viewed from a distance. The result of the mix differs according to the actual type of hue. Warm colours dominate cool. For example, a very small proportion of red dots on a blue field could end up dominating a larger proportion of blue, creating a mauve. This affects colour matching of materials from a distance.

Pictogram An element of signage which describes a word with a very simple picture which everyone should recognise. "Female toilet" would therefore be an outline of a woman. There are internationally agreed pictograms for a wide range of purposes such as accessibility. The use of pictograms attempts to overcome language and cognitive barriers.

Powder coating A process for coating metal objects by the electrical charge of the object which attracts fine particles of coloured powder that coat the metal. A heating process melts the powder to make the coating tough and permanent.

Reflectance The ratio of the amount of light reflected from a surface to the amount of light falling on it. The light reflectance value can be expressed as a decimal (0–1) or percentage (0% to 100%).

Sans-serif Text or typeface without serifs. An example of a typeface with a serif is Times, and without or sans-serif is Arial. Sans-serif typefaces are more easily legible for people with low vision.

Saturation The subjective estimation of the amount of pure, chromatic colour present in a sample, judged in proportion to its brightness. With paints, a hue-like orange might be a highly saturated colour of full strength such as a bright orange or a full colour strength and low lightness value such as a brown or a low saturation and high lightness which would be a pastel peach colour.

Spectrophotometer A hand-held or bench-top device for measuring colour as a CIELab measurement. The measurement plots the colour with a three-dimensional reference point in colour space.

Tactile information Raised areas on signage, buttons or tactile paving; designed for touch sensitivity. Braille is one form of tactile information.

Transmittance [of light through glass] The ratio of the amount of light transmitted inside through the glass to the amount of light incident on its outside. The value can be expressed as a decimal (0–1) or percentage (0% to 100%).

Value In the Munsell System, an index of the lightness of a surface ranging from 0 (black) to 10 (white), in NCS from 0 to 100%. Approximately related to percentage reflectance R by:

$$R = V(V - 1)$$

where V = value.

Visual noise The level of diverse visual material or stimuli which occupies a section of the visual field. Can refer to the visually chaotic clutter of the environment or the lack of control in the display of objects or customised signage.

5.5 Figures

Photographs and illustrations are copyright of or have been supplied by either BRE or the Colour Design Research Centre, except where indicated in the text. Special thanks go to the hospital research teams throughout the NHS trust healthcare establishments visited, who supplied photographs to be used for this report and are credited in the text. We are grateful to the architects who kindly sent photographs of their work for us to use in the report. Care has been taken to ensure that copyright of all figures has been acknowledged without omissions.

Figures 1.1 – 2.20 CDRC SBU; 2.21 – 2.22 CIELAB; 2.23 CDRC SBU; 2.24 PANAZ TEXTILES; 2.25 – 2.81 CDRC SBU; 2.82 PANAZ TEXTILES; 2.83 – 2.84 CDRC SBU; 2.85 – 2.89 NHS ESTATES; 2.90 CDRC SBU; 3.1 – 3.3 BRE; 3.4 CDRC SBU; 3.5 BRE; 3.6 CDRC SBU; 3.7 – 3.12 BRE; 3.13 CDRC SBU; 3.14 BRE; 3.15 CDRC SBU; 3.16 – 3.18 BRE; 4.1 – 4.9 CDRC SBU; 4.10 – 4.11 NHS ESTATES; 4.12 – 4.20 CDRC SBU; 4.21 NHS ESTATES; 4.22 CDRC SBU; 4.23 E. ALLCHURCH; 4.24 BRE; 4.25 CDRC SBU; 4.26 NHS ESTATES; 4.27 – 4.31 CDRC SBU; 4.32 POOLE NHS; 4.33 – 4.44 CDRC SBU; 4.45 BRE; 4.46 TOMMY GOVERN; 4.47 – 4.50 CDRC SBU; 4.51 BRE; 4.52 – 4.60 CDRC SBU; 4.61 BRE; 4.62 CDRC SBU; 4.63 BRE; 4.64 CDRC SBU; 4.65 POOLE NHS; 4.66 – 4.67 CDRC SBU; 4.68 BRE; 4.69 – 4.76 CDRC SBU; 5.1 BRE; PAGE 111 NHS ESTATES; 5.2 – 5.3 BRE

CDRC, LSBU
Colour Design Research Centre, London South Bank University
(From November 2003 the Colour Design Research Group has been based at Kingston University, Kingston, Surrey KT1 2QJ)
BRE
Building Research Establishment

About NHS Estates guidance and publications

The Agency has a dynamic fund of knowledge which it has acquired over 40 years of working in the field. Our unique access to estates and facilities data, policy and information is shared in guidance delivered in four principal areas:

Design & Building

These documents look at the issues involved in planning, briefing and designing facilities that reflect the latest developments and policy around service delivery. They provide current thinking on the best use of space, design and functionality for specific clinical services or non-clinical activity areas. They may contain schedules of accommodation. Guidance published under the headings Health Building Notes (HBNs) and Design Guides are found in this category.

Examples include:

HBN 54, Facilities for cancer care centres
HBN 28, Facilities for cardiac services
Diagnostic and Treatment Centres: ACAD, Central Middlesex Hospital – an evaluation
HFN 30, Infection control in the built environment: design and planning

Engineering & Operational (including Facilities Management, Fire, Health & Safety and Environment)

These documents provide guidance on the design, installation and running of specialised building service systems and also policy guidance and instruction on Fire, Health & Safety and Environment issues. Health Technical Memoranda (HTMs) and Health Guidance Notes (HGNs) are included in this category.

Examples include:

HTM 2007, Electrical services supply and distribution
HTM 2010, Sterilization: operational management with testing and validation protocols
HTM 2040, The control of legionellae in healthcare premises – a code of practice
HTM 82, Fire safety – alarm and detection systems

Procurement & Property

These are documents which deal with areas of broad strategic concern and planning issues, including capital and procurement.

Examples of titles published under this heading are:

Estatecode
How to Cost a Hospital
Developing an Estate Strategy
Sustainable Development in the NHS

NHS Estates Policy Initiatives

In response to some of the key tasks of the NHS Plan and the Modernisation Agenda, NHS Estates has implemented, project-managed and monitored several programmes for reform to improve the overall patient experience. These publications document the project outcomes and share best practice and data with the field.

Examples include:

National standards of cleanliness for the NHS
NHS Menu and Recipe Books
Sold on Health

The majority of publications are available in hard copy from:

The Stationery Office Ltd
PO Box 29, Norwich NR3 1GN
Telephone orders/General enquiries 0870 600 5522
Fax orders 0870 600 5533
E-mail book.orders@tso.co.uk
http://www.tso.co.uk/bookshop

Publication lists and selected downloadable publications can be found on our website:
http://www.nhsestates.gov.uk

For further information please contact our Information Centre:
e-mail: nhs.estates@doh.gsi.gov.uk
tel: 0113 254 7070